DANIEL HABIF

THE UNBREAKABLES

HarperCollins
Leadership

An Imprint of HarperCollins

Published by HarperCollins Leadership, an imprint of HarperCollins Focus LLC, 501 Nelson Place, Nashville, TN 37214, USA.

ISBN 978-1-4002-5485-9 (ePub)
ISBN 978-1-4002-5484-2 (TP)

HarperCollins Publishers, Macken House, 39/40 Mayor Street Upper, Dublin 1, D01 C9W8, Ireland (https://www.harpercollins.com)

Library of Congress Cataloging-in-Publication Data
Library of Congress Cataloging-in-Publication application has been submitted.

Cover design: Sandoval Design & Marketing
Author photos: Ram Martinez

Printed in the United States of America
25 26 27 28 29 LBC 5 4 3 2 1

Table of Contents

Dedication

To Jesus Christ, my greatest love and inspiration; with you everything, without you nothing. Your grace is enough for me.

Anyhita, new worlds are created when I take you by the hand. I love you, and I will always love you. You are my champion.

Mom, you are my superhero. I will write an entire book just to say thank you.

Dad, I would never have made it without you. We will see each other in the eternal.

Brothers, I love you. Remember those nights when we would all sleep together in Acacias #60? Well, I think about them every day.

In-laws and brothers-in-law, I didn't turn out so bad after all. 😬 Cheers, for those afternoons in 701, 402, and 104.

César, Papa Bear, for doing the impossible, for what you've always done, for us, for the *valet parking*, and for the sunflower seeds.

Vanna and Rocco, I leave our friendship etched here. Gñones.

Abraham, God agreed to give me the brother I asked for a long time ago.

Rodolfo, I know this will be the first and only book you will ever read in your life. 😆 I love you, dummy. Twenty years living according to the flesh.

Mario, finally! We have learned to celebrate.

Erika, Lindy, Martita, Nayelli, Cuitlahuac, Fernando, Rolando, Paco, Pepe, R. Chagoya. 🙌 I love you all so much.

To my little kitties, who... are gdhekfixk stepping on the ljyu#% keyboard as I write that I love them.

To everyone who has been with me, regardless of the time and place of the journey, who has shared or commented on a video, a piece of writing, or a photo. To those who have come to a conference, who have hugged me in a restaurant, on the street, in an airport, in a *lobby*, somewhere. To those of you who have sent me an email full of blessings, who have told me never to stop, who have prayed for me. Who have defended me, who have questioned me, who have taught me and given me correction.

To you, who through your love and honor have given me so much joy and happiness. This book is dedicated to you. Without you, I would not be here.

Dedications are very difficult to write when so many people have a place in your heart.

Unbreakable today, tomorrow, and forever. I really do love you all. God bless you.

The End

WARNING:

Lack
of
courage

leads
to
fewer
great
experiences

Before we begin

And I have saved the last page for you. If you want to complete this book, you can finish it off yourself. If you just want to check it off your need-to-do list, you can move on to the next thing.

Or, if you want to start over, not a new book, but a new life, an adventure, then stay and let's create something together. The words contained in this book belong to both of us, because with each rereading you will give the book a new ending. Return to these words as the eternal learner you need to be, because they are not here for you to enhance the brilliance of your intellect, but to enhance the strength of your spirit.

I didn't write this book with the intention of captivating you, on the contrary, I wrote it so that each page would make you want to put it down, to bookmark it, and go out and pursue what resonates within you. When you come back, the bookmark will be where you left it, but you will have changed and become closer to your dreams. I place it in your hands, ready to bear the smudges from the ink and the stains from the coffee, and tears that will be left on its folded pages.

This book contains no abstracts, it is not one of those books that you just strike off as job done and move on to something else. It is not a trophy, not a how-to manual, not a thesis, and not an academic text. If your intention is to go through the book without doing the work yourself, it won't be of any benefit to you. You will recuperate the money that you spent on this book, but the time spent reading it will be gone forever.

The beauty of the book is not in its words, but in the actions that will be generated from reading them. It is composed of a thousand parts of me, loose fragments of my soul and of my flesh: a fortress built from all the stones that have been thrown in my direction, and a crown made from all the gems that I have received. You will find loneliness and joy, yearnings and anxieties, worries and hopes, cries and whispers. It was not easy to let them go.

Letting go hurts, but what does holding on do to us?

I need you to do your part and let go of the stones and pearls that you have received, and use them to build the lighthouse to illuminate others, because this is not a self-help book, it is a book about how to help others. If you don't act upon the words of this book, reading it a hundred times will be of no benefit; you won't really have gotten past the first page until you are able to get someone to stand up and take hold of your arm, only then will you gain the strength to stand on your own two feet.

It is not a treatise intended for the reader to find meaning in everything: it is an invitation to find meaning in everything in life, and for life to have meaning in everything. It is not a recipe book; it is a tribute to the voracious appetite of a crazy dreamer. It does not weave hypotheses, it unravels mysteries; it does not contain doctrines, it connects spirits and opens hearts.

This is not a book about intentions, it is a book about taking action.

Therefore, I ask that when someone lets you into their heart, you first take off your shoes, because the heart is the sanctuary of sacred spaces. I too come barefoot, because I also want you to let me into your heart. But I do not come alone, I will enter with the hand of someone who transcends the finite, who comes from a place that yearns for nothing. He is fulfillment, the greatest restorer of souls. Do not be afraid of Him, for those who open the door to Him will always be fulfilled. He turns houses into homes and seeds into sweet fruits.

My job is not to instruct you, but to show you. Nobody has mastery over your life besides you. Only you know the breadth of your dreams, the dimension that opens when you close your eyes. You are not here to read; you are here to do.

Here you are, the one who takes action. I will accompany you, I will tell you about the countless occasions when I woke up with a smile on my face, my heart intact, and my spirit hardened.

The ideas and concepts that you will find in this book come from a broad range of readings, the result of many hours of study, reflection, and profound observation. Among these sources are the books that comprise the universal literature, that wellspring of timeless wisdom that offers answers to every dimension of thought. I drew the inspiration for this joint endeavor from my mother's words on the day I told her "I'm going to be a billionaire", and she replied "You will be a billionaire the day you have helped a billion people". Together we will pay millions into that account.

This book is here to help you understand that you don't need to feel pressure if, at 25, you haven't found the partner of your dreams, to persuade you that, if you have spent all your life working hard to provide for your family, you can still graduate at 50. In the life that you will build after turning that final page that says "The End," you will no longer feel down because all of your friends have children and you don't, or because you haven't achieved economic independence, or because you haven't been to Paris, or because you don't wear a luxury watch; instead you will fight to achieve it. You will write a new being into life, a new being who ignores those who want you to believe that you should endure something you don't like because others think you should have a car or a yacht. In this new story you no longer live in the shadows of others, because you know that what you want has a price, and you will pay for it with the joy of doing what passionately stirs your soul.

You are the star in your own story, not a carbon copy from other stories.

Let's begin the best chapters of your journey through this life. If you don't like the story you are writing, don't turn the page, change your book completely; and if you love it, then add to its content. I want to thank you for being willing to start this journey, because you have decided to persevere and to dream of changing the world for the better. The best sentence is the one that starts with "Thank you," so I hope these words will serve you and those close to you in a profound way.

We will rediscover your infinite inner potential, your unique qualities, what it is that sets you apart from all that exists throughout the vastness of the cosmos. We will show that we are *Unbreakable*.

Unbreakable is what you and I are.

UN BREAK ABLE «

They are afraid, but they don't stay afraid. They don't put limits on their dreams because they know that there's no such thing as failure, they know that what is gone is no longer needed and what is needed is yet to come. They don't say: "See you tomorrow", because there is no tomorrow.

They seek greatness and don't ask permission to achieve it, they don't have the life that they have been given, they have the life that they have chosen. They know that nothing is permanent: neither mistakes nor fears; they know that no one can steal their dreams, they take risks, they conquer, they construct with their words what they want to see with their eyes.

They don't sigh about things, they sweat for them, they drive out bitterness, rid themselves of anger, and leave folly behind; they know a lot, but they do more. They remain consistent and persevering, they use all their talents and gifts, they don't tolerate mediocrity, they don't waste their time, they raise their standards;

they are not like before,

they accept their mistakes, but they don't dwell on them, they aren't held back by the opinions of others.

The favorite game is the impossible.

They are organized, they don't have a view, they have a vision; when they fall down, they get back up. They turn no into yes, what they want to read about tomorrow, they write today with actions:

UN BREAK ABLE

**forgive,
serve,
love,**

they don't have a
plan B

they don't get to the
top on their own.

They are meek, but not fools, they are forged in fire and pain, they have wept and suffered, they don't lick their wounds, they don't avenge or punish.

They are broken and torn. They aren't holy or perfect.

»

*They are
Unbreakable.*

CRAZY PEOPLE KNOW HOW TO LIVE.

THEY KNOW THAT NOTHING IS PERMANENT, NEITHER MISTAKES NOR FEARS.
THEY KNOW THAT NOBODY CAN STEAL THEIR DREAMS.

THE UNBREAKABLE
ARE BROKEN AND TORN.
THEY ARE NOT PERFECT

THEY TURN NO INTO YES

Chapter 1

A billion hugs

*There is more joy in giving than
in receiving. (Acts 20:35)*
Jesus of Nazareth

There are thousands of self-help books, but not many books on how to help others. The only way to help yourself is by learning how to reach out to others.

You should ask the question, "How can I help you?" to someone every day. How many times have you asked someone that today? Helping someone shouldn't be a chore, it should be a pleasure.

If you use your gifts and talents so that no one lacks:	*I promise you, you will never go without:*
✓ Food	✓ Food
✓ Shelter	✓ Shelter
✓ Clothes	✓ Clothes
✓ Compassion	✓ Compassion
✓ Respect	✓ Respect
✓ Dignity	✓ Dignity
✓ Justice	✓ Justice
✓ Help	✓ Help
✓ Love	✓ Love

It is not about reward; it is about growing in spirit. That is when you will start to reap the benefit from your enrichment.

I hope that when you read this book you keep your radar locked on the impact that you can make. Starting with your immediate surroundings, never forgetting the contribution you will be able to make to millions of people. Together, I want us to build a synergy, inspiring in you an abundance of thought, leading to other fortunes within your household, your street, your neighborhood, your city, exponentially, even throughout the world.

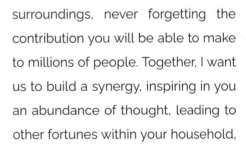

When you don't have, give, and you will see how much you have left over.

This is what it means to be unbreakable. Through your daily action you will be able to use this book to heal wounds, to motivate

If you are tired
of starting

over,

stop
giving
up.

everyone to *keep on pushing* beyond the limits of their known virtues and talents.

Since you've turned the page that says "THE END", you're not in any hurry. Explore these passages for as long as it takes, no one is pressing you for time. I invite you to meditate deeply on their essence, to do what they invite you to do, to engage with them honestly, and not just complete each task without learning from their deeper meaning.

In life, direction is more important than speed.

There are many people who start a book and do not read beyond the first two chapters, but you have already finished this book, so you can continue to reflect without haste. I want you to approach the exercise in a different way, not so much to learn as to teach, not so much to absorb as to radiate, and be an agent of the wonder that neighborly love is able to achieve.

I urge you to read with care and diligence, to interact with the text with integrity and courage. Ruminate on what has already been written, and even more so on what you yourself write.

Since we're writing this book together, it's time for me to introduce myself and tell you a little about who I am. As we were writing, I came across this photograph, and upon seeing it, I was struck for a few minutes, speechless; it was as if the present had punched me right between the eyes, blinding me and opening up the peripheral dimension of my spirit. The most primitive emotions of my soul had been stirred.

Four years before this photograph was taken, in 1988, a twist of fate had led me to take my first steps into the world of entertainment. That day I accompanied my brother Eduardo to the filming of a TV commercial that he and another child were due to star in; it was then that the spirits aligned in my favor: the child who had been selected to play the role of my brother's brother had been taken ill. The producers asked my mother if I could audition, and I ended up playing the role of that boy. Sometimes even catching a cold can be life-altering. Everything happens for the best, as long as we adopt the right attitude.

There I was, right where God had placed me as a tiny piece in an immense game of chess. He already had the opening, and the winning move that would lead to the checkmate of my life.

Photo by Delia Habif Gregoire (1991)

Without knowing it, that day I had started a career, a journey with its small and mediocre achievements, its great failures and its disappointments.

My journey has been one of study and preparation, with very few hours of downtime. While others were kicking a ball around, I was either performing at a forum or helping my mother prepare the sandwiches that I used to sell at school. There were many reasons and shortcomings that prevented me from going to college, so I decided to make a different kind of commitment. My colleagues were reaching their goals in just one step, whereas it was taking me five steps, and I was shattered. Even so, I maintain that there are those who certify their education with diplomas, and others who are certified by life: I studied dance, acting, singing, design, archery, pantomime, ninjutsu, chess, tourism, advertising, painting, and photography. Today, I am devoted to books on apologetics, theology, biology, history, cooking, art, architecture, and any other literature that crosses my path and broadens my horizons, I serve it to myself as food. I will never stop learning and never stop being hungry. I always thought I wouldn't get there, that I wouldn't make it, that I wasn't very smart; I never got great results, I always had to work twice as hard as those who seemed to effortlessly earn the best grades. I lived around rich and well-to-do people, when they ordered a bottle, I had to buy just one beer for myself and make it last the whole night.

After that commercial I did some acting, singing, and some dancing, in everything from musicals to classical theater. I have performed Calderón de la Barca, I have played characters by Luis G. Basurto, Lorca, Argüelles, Chekhov, Dostoyevsky, Grotowski, and Peter Brook. Benedetti would rock me to sleep, I would fly away with Neruda, and Leonardo da Vinci would hypnotized me, while the

Divine Comedy ended up changing my direction completely. I ended up getting drunk with Oliverio Girondo, and Juan Rulfo awakened me with the book *El llano en llamas* (*The Burning Plain*).

Then I began to question everything, starting with Darwin, and my whole life changed when I came across the Bible: Paul had an impact on me with his strength and courage; Solomon taught me about vanity, and how nothing is worth more than wisdom; David showed me that faith brings down giants; Daniel showed me what faithfulness is; and from Moses I learned that there is no such thing as too old to conquer, that even if you stutter, your words have the power to make an impact.

When I read about the walk of Jesus, I fell in love with His footsteps. Following His path, I wrote, composed songs, poems, prose, and phrases that only my mother and I enjoyed, out of sheer commitment.

I formed a *rock* and *funk* band, with whom I recorded an album that was never released, I sang in bars, nightclubs, and places where nobody ever saw me. I dreamed of being the bad boy of music, I was out of tune a thousand times and I will be out of tune a thousand times more.

I was a solo artist but it didn't work out, I produced and directed, I was an ice cream man, and I handed out flyers for my business. I sold food, I had a small factory that I wasn't able to finish, I made thousands, I made millions, and I lost it all; I made millions again, and I lost it all again. They laughed at me, they applauded me, they judged me, I made mistakes, they lied to me, I lied to them, I borrowed money, I lent money and never got it back, they stole from me, they humiliated me, I got angry with God, I still fight with God, and obviously I always lose, they dazzled me and broke my heart, but finally I fell in love, I landed a queen, a princess, I found myself an *amazing woman*.

I got married; it was tough to win her over, but almost two decades later I'm still with her, my best friend and my partner in everything.

To be bacteria and infect me is to fail as bacteria.

✅

Besides that, I had a nightclub that I also lost, but I had fun in the meantime; I put on more than 600 concerts, I produced hundreds of marketing campaigns, I employed hundreds of people. By the time I was 27, I had sold thousands of tickets as a show promoter.

I was ambitious, greedy, egomaniacal, and I still am a little today (okay... a lot). That's why life ended up beating me to the ground. I tried to be a talent manager, and I succeeded. I lost my company, built a new one, and lost it again. People hired me, I was an employee, then I was a boss, then an owner, and in the end I was nothing.

I lost my father, and I lost my friends and associates. I lost, and I lost again, and I will continue to lose, but none of these losses took away my passion, my grit, and my tenacity. I was given a life and a body, and I'm going to use it all, I'm not going to leave anything behind.

I suffered from Lyme disease, I lost my memory, I felt like I was dying and I almost did die. I was sick for five years and underwent treatment for two years, I also suffered from insomnia and delirious fevers.

But I didn't go it alone, many have helped me along the way: my wife, my mother, my brothers, my manager, my team, my friends, my employees, my partners, my enemies, and my detractors have all played their part over the years. I cannot thank or honor enough those people who reached out to me when I had nothing, or those who pushed me to the point of falling to my knees. No one gets to the top alone; usually loneliness accompanies us on our way back when we descend from the summit.

If my future self could come back, it would say something like:

Hey Daniel! Don't get yourself down anymore. The future looks good, really good, better than you can imagine. But before then, I will put you through the fire and the wilderness, you are going to want to take your own life a couple of times, you will go to a psychologist and they will tell you that you don't fit into society. They will prescribe you pills for hyper-activity and people will freak out at your intensity and pas-sion. You will walk around in solitude for hours and scream so loudly inside that the windows of your soul will start to break. And even so, no one is going to come and help you.

But rest assured, because you will come out of it unbreakable: all the terrors you will experience will be levers with which to raise up a generation of love and peace. Your pain will be turned into joy, because from suffering comes the warmth of a smile that will adorn your face, and the smile will be formed from the wounds that you will have learned to repair.

Have faith, because God will give you the most beautiful woman, she will be the love of your life and you will embark on challenging adventures together. Get ready, because both young and old will listen to the messages that will pour from your heart, you will raise the fallen, fill theaters, and write books. Your passion will set the coals of others aflame, you will help children and the elderly, you will bind marriages, reconcile nations, be persecuted and take much criticism, you will become sick, people who you love will die, you will continue to suffer betrayal, and people will try to rob you of your blessings. But your steadfastness will be such that no one will be able to stop you, because everything you believe will be orientated around God, like a child, and your flame will burn so brightly in preparation for you to be entirely consumed by His love.

You will be a kind of countercurrent, but neither rain, nor storm, nor desert will shake your will when it comes to serving the King.

Your epitaph will read: "Here lie a billion hugs."

God willing, I will return a discarded suit to Him and when He asks me: "What is this?" I will say: "Forgive me Lord, but you told me to believe you, and so I believed everything". And I will give up to Him a body that will no longer be usable by anyone, because it will only fit my own scratches and wounds, I will have patched up my scars and fixed up my tears. I will return to you a suit that looks like it has been trampled over by a hundred buffaloes and chewed by a thousand hyenas, but with a smile that can never be erased, because it confounded terror whenever terror came knocking.

Now I want you to tell me something about yourself. Tell me, if your future self could come back, What would it tell you? What will your epitaph say?

LETTER FROM
YOUR FUTURE SELF

CREATE DREAMS | OVERCOME OBSTACLES | WHAT WOULD YOU SAY TO YOURSELF? | HOW FAR DID YOU GE

#00001

YOUR
EPITAPH
WILL SAY:

YOUR PLEDGE TAKES NO TIME AT ALL

Young people and entrepreneurs who have squandered their motivation on fear and doubt, have allowed the opinions of the envious, the realists, and the dogmatists to hollow out their minds and their spirits, they have allowed them to hold them back.

If you no longer dream, at least stop killing the dreams of others. Life is not a 100-meter sprint, it is an endurance race: more than a party, it is an incredible desert, in which you need more character and temperament than talents or gifts.

The challenge of the century is to do more with what we know. I promise you that this will open up paths in the desert and rivers in the wilderness. You will experience these words merely as an injection of enthusiasm that will last for a few hours or a few days, and then the excitement will subside and you will be thrown back into confusion or depression due to a lack of purpose.

If your dreams don't terrify you, it's because you're still aiming too low. Dream until your legs tremble.

You will experience this motivation as an act of magic and not as an irreversible part of your life. You must engrave your soul, reprogram your mind and your heart with the codes from our Lord, you must urgently clean out the cobwebs of mediocrity and elevate yourself to a new standard. Make a vow to yourself wherever you are, make a vow right now, realize that it's not that you really want to change, it's just that you would like to change; it's not that you really want to stop being depressed, it's just that you would like to stop being depressed; what you have is a list of desires, not a list of convictions.

No desire exists without the firm power of decision and action, but before we can learn, we have to unlearn. Throw away that which you know no longer serves you; you need strength, not rigidity. Your pledge will not be postponed, not even for a single day, you must understand that this commitment is yours, and belongs solely to you, and you must be willing to fight for it.

You will soon be amazed at how things you thought were lost will come to fruition, but you must be willing to work hard and stay motivated. The Lord expects you to walk and believe. Even with the little He has told you so far, and even if you don't see it, you cannot refute it. This is the faith that lives in you and in me, the faith that is no longer a mere concept, it is the faith that surpasses the natural; many accomplishments arise when you reach a point where you feel unable to continue, when both your mind and body are exhausted. At that point, you return to faith.

Remember how much progress you have made, instead of focusing on what you have not yet achieved. You're not where you want to be, but you're not where you used to be either.

Wait, and by that, I mean learn to wait. Knowing how to wait is an art that requires the adoption of an attitude and the exercise of faith; everyone needs faith: doctors, engineers, designers, producers, entrepreneurs, artists, painters, inventors, architects, atheists, agnostics, astrologers, we all need faith. Waiting only brings impatience to people who do not have active faith.

Strengthen your faith and close the doors to doubt. Faith is the cure and the antidote to "failure" and

Practice faith intensely and nothing will be impossible.

depression, it is stronger than time and more definitive than death, it is the basis of all miracles and mysteries that cannot be analyzed through logic and science. Faith contradicts and humbles logic; in faith you discover the never-ending source of life. Faith gives you purpose and makes you invincible.

Do you remember the prayer you prayed a long time ago, and that you no longer pray because you think it will not come to pass? I promise you that you will see it with your own eyes: the tears that have been shed, and that broken heart will be rewarded.

I have lived it, this is my experience. I promise you, you'll see it.

Believe me!

Chapter 2

Let's become traffickers

Not too smart, not too dumb. I was what
I was: a mixture of vinegar and olive oil.
A sausage of both angel and beast!

Nicanor Parra

I hope the letter you received from the future has brought you great revelations. We have only just started; the person you will become is helping somebody already.

However, there are still a few things I need to know about you before we continue on our path. I want to know how much we have in common, so I ask you to write in the spaces I have provided, with the utmost honesty, the five things you love most about this life:

Now I want you to look at the list and see if it includes you.

I ASKED
HIM TO MENTION
THINGS HE LOVES

AND HE NEVER MENTIONED
HIS NAME.

If you haven't included yourself, then you have a lot to think about. Imagine what this means: you live with yourself 100% of the time, for goodness' sake, and you're not on the list of what you love the most?

You must like something about yourself, it is important that you reflect on what those things are. It is not wrong to appreciate your own virtues. You shouldn't be ashamed if you like your hair, how well you dance, or the tone of your voice. Indulge in how you draw, how well you cook, or what a good father you are.

We were taught not to be believed, to discard the idea that we could achieve something great, that applause was reserved for geniuses, for stars, for those who had accomplished great feats. We have been educated to apologize for our achievements. We were taught to be quiet, not to ask, not to interrupt, to follow the rules.

Next time you make plans, don't forget to include yourself.

Society, culture, tradition, and family would always put a muzzle on us whenever, sitting at the table, we dared to confess our dreams. Exploring our own abilities would make us smug, and we learned that it was only polite to assume the excessive modesty under which our talents remained hidden; we did it so as not to intimidate, so that our little brother wouldn't cry, so that our boss wouldn't feel threatened, so that our husband wouldn't feel uncomfortable by the side of a woman of such virtue.

They judged us and buried us on the spot. After hiding our talents, we were then asked to do the same with our anxieties: "Don't fantasize so much", "don't waste your time on that", "don't chase the impossible". "Don't ...", "don't ...", "don't ...". They became weary from continuously telling us: "Don't be what you are." Discovering who you are, accepting who you are, and being who you are, comes at a very high price, but it is the price of human dignity, even more so when society prefers when you are not your true self.

Receive. Receiving is also part of who we are. We have been taught not to accept compliments: They tell you that you look good and you say: "What do you mean, look at my belly?" When they congratulate you, you say: "It was nothing, I still have so much to learn." We were taught to give, but not to receive. This devalues us, it puts us out of sync. We must embrace a healthy level of self-esteem that allows us to give and receive, based on spiritual values, even if they are radical or uncomfortable for society. People who have low self-esteem do not know how to receive and therefore find it difficult to give; they are ashamed to celebrate their triumphs and do not appreciate the triumphs of others.

Believing that we are not capable of being good at something is not the same as believing that we are stupid. Saying that you don't like your nose is not the same as saying that you are hideous. Everything that we consider to be part of our identity has a profound and immediate impact on us. Therefore, when you change your beliefs about your identity, you return to your original model and become the person you really are.

Our beliefs are constructed by what we have been told, our experience, the books we have read, and the things we have seen, the influence of our teachers, partners, parents, as well as the prevailing culture and media. All this has an impact on our mental and spiritual world, it ends up rooted in the conscious and subconscious, etched into our spirit. That is why beliefs are buried deep in our mind and seem very difficult to access.

We need to understand where our negative thoughts come from, what triggers them and thus prevent them from reappearing, but because they are deep-seated beliefs, we cling to them repeatedly. Self-esteem allows us to continuously improve ourselves and, above all, it pushes us to empower and motivate others.

Being yourself in a world where most people don't want to be themselves is a resounding success.

We should seek the testimony of our own self-assessment, which inspires and breaks with the *status quo* and with false modesty. We desperately need to stop destroying aspirations in our educational system, homes, and businesses.

You can start by being who you really are, and you will soon see the doors thrown wide open. Do not pretend that you are someone else or believe that you are less, because we all have the same value, even if we are different. Seek to eliminate blame, ridiculous demands, perfectionism, and the need to win at any cost.

If you ever lose someone because of your own introspection, because your soul overflows, because you love too much, or because you take the risk to challenge and confront, to raise your voice in the face of injustice, being true to your convictions, or because you said no, not yielding to compromise, because you put yourself out there as you are, or because you simply showed your faith, you will not have lost, you will have won.

Indeed, I'm not asking you to believe that you are the most important thing in the world, I'm just asking you to learn to respect yourself and to appreciate the qualities that you have in you.

Go back through the exercise on page 38, and if you still don't include yourself in the list of what you love most, we have a lot of growing to do. Don't worry, you will learn to love yourself. When God is at the top of that list, so too will you be.

The unbreakable use all their talents and gifts, something that is only possible when you appreciate that these talents and gifts reside in you. But we must remember that our main mission is to get others to unleash their own attributes.

Our educational system spends a lot of time teaching children how to obtain wealth, but it does not teach them why they should want it, how to enjoy it, or, much less, how to use it wisely. We leave school knowing mathematics, chemistry, and history,

If you think you are the greatest in the world, maybe your world is too small.

but without knowing how to speak in public, how to relate to others, or how to understand the tribes that live together in our cities. Teachers motivate, but they do not inspire. No country offers classes on emotional intelligence. There are no subjects in the curriculum on how to manage and master emotions, there is no ministry dedicated to self-esteem. And we will talk about this more.

Since we have been taught to repress our self-esteem and we are not taught to develop it in schools, we have no choice but to act like people who harbor underhanded ideas or deal in illicit substances. We should act as members of an underground cell, as operators who disseminate dangerous ideas.

The stereotype has always been that Hispanics are traffickers. I suggest that we all become traffickers in self-esteem: my drug of choice. I have the seeds, the ingredients, and the market; I will plant them, water them, and harvest them myself. The seeds will multiply and there will be many left over. It's legal, it does no harm, it can be distributed without prosecution, it helps others, it's pleasantly addictive, it allows for the redemption of souls, and it fuels no sense of sadness. The reward is eternal and is indestructible on Earth, it causes no hangover or side effects, it purifies the environment and enhances human talent. Self-esteem is the only substance that, if we became addicted to it, would wipe out the use of all conventional drugs.

If you want to make a change you should start by changing what you believe.

Self-esteem removes frowns and expels rage, it dispels darkness and brings happiness to you and those around you, it realigns body chemistry, alters genetics, restores vision and focus, and lifts us up in the face of doubt and conflict. Self-esteem fosters healing, brings wisdom and discernment, and places you in the center of a balance between peace and joy, it triggers endorphins and, in the right measure, makes us all more human.

I invite you to traffic in self-esteem and to become addicted to it, to condemn yourself to live in the spirit all of your days. You will hallucinate with it more than with any chemical, and you will see things that no narcotic will ever be able to show you. Go, and be a transgressor of good, and you will gain much more than can ever be gained from evil. Even when you have to overcome challenges, drastic changes, belated promises, painful ordeals, unanswered prayers, unfair criticisms, tragedies, and undeserved blows, never stop doing good.

There is a formula for nurturing self-esteem and planting it in every-one around you. For me, the best way to achieve this is to be close to the people who nourish your soul.

You can't keep company with people who are trying to cheat you.

We usually like to stay close to the nest, where we were taught to fly, and not where our wings are clipped. Therein lies the importance of surrounding ourselves with people who value our talents, not those who despise what we like about ourselves.

Let us also not commit the cruelty of belittling what others value in their own being. If you love someone, but you can't stand what that person loves about him- or herself, you must ask yourself two things: first, whether you really love that person; then you must understand why the thing that is so important to that person hurts you so much.

We live in a world plagued by senseless pain, corrupt govern-ments, political violence, weak economies, and impoverished cultures. Even so, there is something worse that eats away at us, something that has nested in our hearts: greed, revenge, pride, envy, and arrogance are at the epicenter of the earthquake that buried us under its rubble. If we continue on this path, we will be remembered as the generation of turmoil, a generation of insolence, and a gener-ation without stewardship.

There is something tragic and profane in the current state of our hearts; we have blinded our minds and neglected how beautiful we are inside (and even outside); we are wrong to say that we must bring out our human side, we simply need to remember that we have it.

A head of those who

The distractions of everyday life divert our attention from the incomparable beauty that surrounds us and the immense potential that we possess. We no longer discern, we no longer observe, we look but we don't see what we actually are. We perceive without sentiment; we live without feeling alive.

We want to show, to teach, to look for answers, but the answers lie with us, and this is something that we have forgotten. We will not be fertile soil if we fall into the seduction of the superfluous; self-esteem cannot germinate in this kind of soil.

ENVY

ALWAYS

WANTS TO DESTROY

WHAT IT **KNOWS** IS

NOT ITS OWN.

We Latin Americans have become a living contradiction, because at the same time that we get up at 4:30 a.m. and show unwavering determination, we find ourselves distant from reality, at times we numb ourselves, we never believe in ourselves.

These days we know everything except how to be happy.

Never stop, even when it feels like the weight on your shoulders is overwhelming, because that weight will never be too much for the strength of your inner soul. Never let envy take control over your responsibilities.

Envy destroys self-esteem in its wake, so it must be eradicated.

THE ENVIOUS

"Daniel, don't you think that maybe you believe in yourself too much?" I was asked suddenly.

"Could it be, rather, that you think I believe in myself too much because you believe in yourself too little?" I answered.

Your success will be the defeat of mediocrity, believe me. The most compelling evidence of this can be found in the comments section of social media platforms. It's quite frightening to see so much bitterness. It's always "us versus them." On our continent we have seen that it is far easier to rally people against something than to rally them in support of something.

When we judge others, we undermine our own reasoning. Self-esteem cannot be cultivated through random criticism. I read messages from hundreds of people who only engage using offensive language and sarcasm. There are so many people who cannot come up with well-defined positions or articulate facts effectively. They avoid engaging in constructive debate and instead opt to criticize people and try to undermine their credibility.

They take satisfaction from making hurtful remarks, yet are reluctant to face confrontation themselves. Their interpretation of your words is based on their own biases. I have been questioned hundreds of thousands of times about my faith, my passion, the way I dress, the way I write, the way I speak, the way I take photos, where I dine, the

If you have a negative opinion of me without really knowing me, then I promise to make every effort not to disappoint you.

brands I wear, the way I love, the way I serve, even about my passion. Some say that I overdo it, that I use grandiose language, often neglecting to consider the substance of my message. It is incredible how people can exhibit such fervor about things that do not truly interest them.

There are people who hate a TV series, but yet they comment on every episode, every scene. They watch it only so they can write negative comments about it, they take part in things they don't even like just so that they can show their disapproval. What kind of contradictory behavior is this? They visit accounts of people they hate more than they visit their parents.

We all like to wear clothes that fit us, as long as they don't constrict our egos.

In a society where there is a good balance of self-esteem, there is no need for envy. Only someone who has no appreciation for themselves can just sit on the couch criticizing others: "Only now that she's had plastic surgery, she's able to be successful", "She slept with such-and-such a person, and that's why she made it", "That award is rigged", "He's just daddy's boy".

Have you ever made comments like this? Don't tell me, keep your answer to yourself, but if you have, examine what your reasons were for doing so. Why put so much focus on someone else if there is still so much you need to improve in yourself?

"Daniel, I do like your work, but how much longer do you think this motivational speaker fad will last?" he said smiling.

"Oh, that's adorable," I say, "people of an envious nature have been in fashion for centuries. Do the math."

And with that, the smile was gone.

Forty years ago, nobody had a voice, now everyone has a voice. But these days it is better not to say anything at all. Hundreds of geniuses have stayed silent for fear of being attacked; people are so hostile toward thought that now everyone uses viewpoint relativity as an excuse. Maybe you have a different perspective to mine, but what makes the difference is that you will see everything from a different angle. How you interpret something does not change what you are looking at. Just because you think the moon is made of cheese, doesn't mean you can eat it; you may spend your whole life believing you are a horse, but the day you die the record will bear your name.

The judgment of others will never outweigh the grace that supports you.

I might not be able to see your thoughts, but that doesn't mean that I can dismiss them. Be very careful what words come out of your mouth, because once they are spoken, they cannot be taken back. If you spread negativity, you will end up reaping its consequences yourself. If you are being judged, singled out, or facing criticism, it means that you are moving in the right direction.

Why would anyone criticize someone who is pursuing their dreams? Their dreams belong to them, not to you.

If your dreams are being overshadowed by someone else's, maybe it's because yours don't shine brightly enough.

We cannot be traffickers of self-esteem if we indulge in taking away other people's dreams. Envy comes unexpectedly and irrationally, stemming from a soul devoid of belief in its own abilities.

51

—How things have changed, right?

—I think he got fed up of pretending, didn't he?

Stop judging people and stop hiding your talents. Join us in trafficking self-esteem.

Chapter 3

From our outer shell to our innermost core

It is not your business to succeed, but to do right.
When you have done so the rest lies with God.

C. S. Lewis

You have now become a trafficker, and if you traffic self-esteem to those that don't have it, you will start to notice the transformation that takes place in the people around you. This stimulant will gradually take effect on you, and you will see the impact that it has on people who previously shied away from self-reflection.

When people believe in their potential and maintain a healthy self-esteem that does not harm themselves or those around them, success becomes inevitable. However, much more than just talent is required to achieve this; three major additional components are vital. The first of these consists of a relentless discipline and the application of the necessary tools, which we will talk about in later chapters; the second aspect lies in knowing what success means to us, how we can understand it and what we must do to make sure we are on the right track. Spiritual fulfillment is the final ingredient, because without it there is no success at all, neither potential success nor sustainable success.

You may wonder why defining success is so important. The reason is very simple, there are many people who say they want to be *successful*, when really what they want is to be *famous*. We are completely mesmerized by the spotlights. We always believe that as long as we can feel the glow of the *flash* on our face and the burst of the *click* on our ego, we are on the right path. Greed has made us forget the mission.

Greed not only accumulates in our wallets, but also spreads like wildfire in our hearts. Each day we crave more and more validation without understanding why. We have lost sight of our true aspirations and completely forsaken the essence of our dreams.

In my everyday interactions, I encounter an increasing number of individuals from various backgrounds who share a common ambition: they aim for success without expecting failure. These are people who desire the rewards of life without truly experiencing it, seeking spoils without doing the work, they want to feel the sense

-Daniel Habif
get them written down with facts.
phrases about success. It is time to
Enough of repeating nice-sounding
-Daniel Habif
get them written down with facts.
phrases about success. It is time to
Enough of repeating nice-sounding
-Daniel Habif
get them written down with facts.
phrases about success. It is time to
Enough of repeating nice-sounding

Enough of repeating nice-sounding phrases about success. It is time to get them written down with facts.
-Daniel Habif

Enough of repeating nice-sounding phrases about success. It is time to get them written down with facts.
-Daniel Habif

Enough of repeating nice-sounding phrases about success. It is time to get them written down with facts.
-Daniel Habif

Enough of repeating nice-sounding phrases about success. It is time to get them written down with facts.
-Daniel Habif

of victory without going into battle. They want profit, without sales; sales, without strategy; strategy, without knowing the customers; customers, without resources to provide them; resources, without tools; and tools, without expenditure.

There are people who want a degree without studying, they place more value on a diploma hanging on the wall than on the knowledge they have in their heads. We have become fixated on speed, prioritizing making money over the necessary personal and professional development for life, which consists of two components: human and professional preparation.

We want to build a gigantic world, but we are not willing to lay even the tiniest of bricks.

We usually admire what we do not have. Our desires tend to come from a hollow perspective, considering that our shortcomings are greater than our fulfillment. Without a doubt, desire initiates the journey to achieving a dream or a goal, it is the spark that leads to prosperity or the growth of our crops. This desire must be tempered with wisdom; first we need to make a real and objective assessment of our talents and gifts, so that we know where we stand. By doing this, we will be able to draw up a detailed strategy, and we will be ready for the necessary improvisation that comes with the uncertainty of entrepreneurship.

In the previous chapter we stressed the importance of identifying feelings of envy, and above all how to overcome it. We must conduct an honest evaluation of ourselves, since this is one of the many irrational emotions that we have as human beings; it is not your fault if you feel this way, but it will be your fault if you harbor these feelings in your heart, and allow them to rule over your actions.

If you can't bear loneliness, don't seek success.

Admiring a person and being inspired by that person is not the same as wanting what that person has. There is a line, which is almost invisible, separating these two paths, and the outcome of each one is vastly different. To understand whether we admire someone or desire what they have, we need to examine ourselves honestly, but in a way that is not too harsh. Let's look at what we are and what we have. Once we've done this, let's look at the person we admire from an overall perspective. Do we think their life is better than ours because it is full of fancy things?

We have to make a frank assessment of whether we really want these things, but more importantly, whether we really need them. Does our idea of success resemble what that person has achieved? Does it come at a price that we are willing to pay? Will we be happy once we achieve it? And when we achieve it, will we have anything to offer to others?

Many say they want to know the truth, but very few are prepared to face it. "For where your treasure is, there your heart will be also" (Matthew 6:21), Scripture states. Finally, do not rely on the talents and gifts of others, do not misrepresent yourself and never compare yourself to others. Maybe what you believe to be your greatest virtue is a disadvantage to someone else, or vice versa: what many consider to be a disadvantage may be your greatest strength.

Be very clear when defining success; it should be more like a place to which you can lead others, rather than a place to which you arrive on your own. Certainly, you don't need a slimmer waistline, more expensive clothes, a fancier car, or a bigger house in order to be successful. These just represent symbols of power and, as such, do not form part of your identity; although I must admit that they do have a great deal of impact on our society. Cars, designer clothes, and trendy restaurants are nothing more than toys, and I have no problem with toys, as long as you are playing with them and not the other way around. If the toys are playing with you, then you are only interested in appearances.

If there is something missing on the outside, look for it on the inside.

I have said a lot, so now it's your turn: describe your success on pages 60–61. Yes, just as you see it.

Close your eyes; really, close them. There you go... better to close them once you've reviewed your success.

When you close your eyes, imagine living the life that you want. Imagine this image as if you were landing in a city that you have always wanted to visit: admire from the window the contours and landscapes that surround it; as the plane approaches, you can make out its parks and avenues, and when it touches down, you will see, one by one, the sights that you have always wanted to see.

Draw your success in meticulous detail, describing what your house looks like and how many rooms it has, what your company produces and how many people you employ, what kind of music you play and how many Grammy Awards you have won. This concept applies to all your desires.

Finally, don't imagine a future for yourself that is meaningless. I would also like to score a World Cup–winning goal; I can fantasize about it, but being a footballer is not what I aspire to be. You should picture your achievements clearly and consistently, be firm in determining why you want these things in your life and the reason why you want them. It's like buying a car; you don't just go to the dealership and say to the salesperson: "Just give me a car." When you walk in you know which model you want. The same is true of your dreams.

Don't downplay doing the things that are fulfilling to you, not all dreams have to be a path to fame. They don't all have to involve a grandiose vision.

Describe the feelings that run through your body, what are you doing, what can you smell, what sounds do you hear? Do the exercise calmly and with no distractions. We both know that achievements require processes, they don't happen overnight, but imagine, for now, that day has already arrived.

Ensure that you do not underestimate the power of imagination, it is not just a simple exercise, there are many studies and experiments that endorse its practical benefits.

You are here because you have taken the decision to carry out these exercises properly. When you open your eyes and see what that day will be like, in the middle of the page, write down what stood out for you the most. When you have finished, make sure you have provided an answer as to what you were doing, who was with you,

What talents led you there?

Who accompanied you?

What were the stumbling blocks that you had to face?

What did you give up in order to achieve it?

Who did you have to leave behind?

What was the first step, when did you take it and what happened to make you finally do it?

Were you happy along the way?

Your dream

What are the differences between that person and who you are today?

What were you enjoying more? Was it the moment itself, or the surroundings and the toys?

Were you with people you love, people you admire or strangers?

Who did you feel the most gratitude toward? Is God one of them?

Once you had achieved your success, were you able to help others? Did you do it?

Were you happy?

Write down your answers here

Write down your answers here

Your
dream

Will the things that are about to come into my life bring me peace and joy?

Will this bring me closer to my life's purpose?

Do the things I desire serve others?

where in the world it was happening, what your attitude was like, and whether you had *toys* with you or not.

On the left-hand side of the box, you will see an arrow where you can write down everything that happens from today until you reach your goal. Connect with your vision and answer the questions:

- What talents led you there?
- Who accompanied you?
- What stumbling blocks did you face?
- What did you give up in order to achieve it?
- Who did you have to leave behind?
- What was the first step, when did you take it and what happened to make you finally do it?
- Were you happy along the way? I have to emphasize this: Were you happy along the way?

On the right-hand side, follow the other arrow and focus on the version of yourself you saw in your vision:

- What are the differences between that person and who you are today?
- What did you enjoy the most? The moment, the environment, or the toys?
- Were you with people you love, people you admire, or strangers?
- Who did you feel the most gratitude toward? Is God one of them?
- Once you had achieved your success, were you able to help others? And did you?

- Were you happy?

Now answer the following: Do you want success or only the pleasures that come with success?

How you define the center will tell you what you are seeking. The answers on the left-hand side will reveal the price that you will have to pay. What you write on the right-hand side will tell you whether what you want is success or toys, the substance or the show, satisfaction or vanity.

If your definition of success is to become a great dancer, but in your vision you were not dancing, you were driving a Ferrari; if you think of success as being a great entrepreneur, but in your vision you were lounging between two palm trees instead of leading a team, do you think you have come up with the right vision?

Many people say: "If only I had...., it would be such and such", "If only I lived there, it would be different". If, when you ask these questions, your conclusion is that these are things you really need, then your next question needs to be, when am I going to use it, and what am I going to use it for? Once you've got those answers and written them down, then come the key questions:

- Will what I am going to do bring me peace and joy?
- Will this bring me closer to my life's purpose?
- Do the things I desire serve others?

If the answer to these questions is yes, then you already have a large part of the mental and emotional strategy you need to start moving toward your goal. If not, you may need to rethink your definition of success.

Don't worry if your answers elicit fear.

The unbreakable live to be, and not to be seen. One of the things I never understand is when people prioritize the external and justify it to themselves by saying: "Everyone does it", as if conforming to the world somehow equates to conformity with an absolute truth. We forget that the established norm does more harm to the world than cancer itself, because it destroys life and makes us vegetate in the narrow box of conformity. Associating the majority opinion with moral righteousness is akin to assuming that consuming garbage is enjoyable simply because that's what flies do: popularity does not equate to quality.

There are paths that lead to success, but only one that leads to your purpose.

I do not agree with the notion that "if something seems true, then it must be; if it doesn't appear true, then it isn't." Gandhi didn't seem like a typical hero, but he was. The Beatles didn't look like superstars, but yet they were the greatest superstars.

And what about Jesus? He had the appearance of a carpenter, and yet He is the King of kings.

The point is that most people are concerned with *appearances*. If something doesn't appear as it is, then that is not what it is; if it resembles an artist, it is indeed an artist; if it looks like an engineer, it is an engineer. You cannot hold on to a vain idea for the rest of your life, because sooner or later you will see the threads start to fray.

There are those who follow trends, while there are others who set them: the latter are the unbreakable.

SUCCESS

WITHOUT GRATITUDE

WILL SATISFY YOUR HUNGER

BUT NEVER

YOUR HEART.

This is not such a provocative position; rebellion without purpose is pure hypocrisy. I believe in the individual revolution of the mind, the soul, the spirit: the most powerful tools of the human species. Creativity and innovation are the greatest evidence that we are infinite beings, it is our limited expectations that confine and restrict our ideas.

There are no stupid ideas, it is only a matter of time before what was considered nonsense yesterday is hailed as genius tomorrow. There will be thousands of people who will tell you that you are insane, that you are delusional, they will accuse you of being ignorant, naive, incapable.

If you believe in your idea, then stand firm. Obviously, to achieve this you will need strategy, tools, preparation, discipline, and perseverance. But if you allow your idea to die with every shot fired, someone else will seize the opportunity and build upon it. It doesn't matter that you came up with the idea yourself, only those who have the endurance and determination to overcome the conflict and stay the course will be able to firmly establish their goals.

THEY WILL LAUGH AT YOU

Many want to take on the world, but they give up at the first hurdle when the world pushes back. Everyone wants to be successful until they realize that they will be betrayed, criticized, singled out, and crucified; because pointing fingers, criticizing, giving opinions, and judging is easy. The most difficult thing is setting an example.

Many of them will stay with you as long as you do not pose a threat or try to outdo them. Others will want to come along with you for the ride, unable to keep up; sooner or later, they will get tired and try to hold you back. People forgive everything but success.

They will laugh at you, talk about you, and list your *failures* along with all the arguments for why you should not dream. They will spread their negativity on the sidewalks of wasted footsteps, they will scream to those who crave revenge, but so long as they speak, your deeds will crush them, and though they may not say it out loud, they will have no choice but

True success is dying while fulfilling your purpose.

to accept that you risked what they were too afraid to risk, that you never stepped off the path that God carved for you out of the rock.

The unbreakable know how to live in conflict without losing their inner peace, they channel rejection and mockery, they are ready to lose everything without surrender. Priorities become distorted when we focus on achieving success without peace, leading to stress and confusion. You can dedicate every second of your existence trying to live a dignified life, but you won't always be the center of attention. There are times when you shine and times when you need to step back.

Don't put a label on your life until it's time to carve your tombstone. Enjoy adversity and realize the power it has to awaken talents that lie dormant in a false sense of comfort. Be excited by the challenges you face and enjoy the storms, because what doesn't challenge you doesn't transform you.

Have mastery of the role that you have taken on, shine brightly in the spotlight, be recognized in the final credits, but never allow yourself to be mediocre.

Eradicate mediocrity from all areas of your life, this includes limiting your relationship with mediocre people in all their variants: judgmental, fearful, negative, lazy, cowardly, foolish, unfaithful, dogmatic, resentful, bitter, abusive, and constantly late.

Err on the side of boldness, not caution.

All of these vices are contagious. I am not suggesting that you delete your contacts from your phone or stop communicating with them. Rather, I am simply recommending that you limit the time you spend with them and the importance you place on relationships or situations that do not bring blessings or enhance your productivity. We often mimic our surroundings, and before we know it, we realize that we are aboard the same wayward ship. There are only two ways to get to port: you either put them aside and take the helm, or you jump overboard and swim to port.

If you hang around with people who don't understand your purpose, you will end up not understanding it either.

Chapter 4

Make more mistakes

Success is stumbling from failure to failure without losing your enthusiasm.

Winston Churchill

W e have just been talking about success. We have defined success, and established the boundary between your desires and your purpose. We have seen that the formula has many ingredients, two of which are fundamental: the first is faith, and the second is what we call "failure".

You may find it strange that we dedicate a chapter to failure in a book whose goal is to help people achieve their potential, but the fact is that the unbreakable are forged by blows; just because we don't break doesn't mean we don't fall, or that it doesn't hurt.

There are no successful people who have not come from *failure* because that is where our destiny gets defined. I cannot guarantee that I will be successful in whatever I do, but I can assure you that before I am successful, I will have experienced many setbacks.

Having a bad attitude when it comes to success is the worst of failures, but having a good attitude when it comes to failure is the greatest of successes.

When you start at the back, you have to eat dust before getting to the front. Before you start being well paid, you first have to be willing to put in much more effort and get paid less than your talents deserve. Before you sell your art, you will first be sold by your friends. Before you love, you will first be betrayed. Before you discover yourself, you will first be lost. Before you receive affection, you will first experience betrayal. Before becoming an oasis, you will first be a desert. Before you are thunder, you will be only rain, and before you feel alive, you will feel dead. Before you know God, you will know evil. Before you become big, you will be the smallest of your tribe. Before being everything, you will live with nothing.

Before loving your dreams, learn to love your wounds. Before you roar, you will feel fear in the darkness of the jungle. Before you fly, you will walk with those who crawl, because for a star to be born, it must first explode. Without implosion there is no light, without brokenness there is no wisdom. The most beautiful smile is the one that has experienced pain, the one that explodes from deep within, the brave warrior in the journey of life.

Ignite those that are dead inside but have not yet been buried.

The challenge is not to avoid "failure", the challenge is to get back up after failure. Those who are truly successful do not relent, they do not give up; they keep pushing themselves even when faced with challenges; overcoming obstacles and never staying down. There is no such thing as failure; what we have is the idea of feeling like a failure. That feeling only permeates your mind when you allow it to. This is why I don't call it "failure", rather *a list of experiences*. It is okay to make mistakes, but it is important not to repeat them. Stand up, overcome your fear, don't hesitate, and don't fold in the face of rejection. Don't try to please everyone; if you only want to please others, you are rejecting yourself.

Some people give up for no reason whatsoever.

When you constantly encounter the *feeling of failure*, you may start to believe that your efforts are not worth it, leading to feelings of discouragement and a belief that trying again is not worth it. We apply that conjecture to everything—business, relationships, projects—but it is only when we stumble upon it that we need to stop, take a cautious step back, and try again.

Fear of failure is one of the worst fears there is, because it prevents us from receiving the plethora of blessings that can come from a fall. Without failure, we cannot reach our destination, because the only people who fall are the ones moving forward.

If I'm already on the ground, it's easier for me to get to my knees.

If you have the courage to pursue your dreams, I assure you that you will fall. When that happens, get back on your feet, but before you do, take a moment to appreciate the tones of the asphalt and the coldness of the concrete. Pray: by kneeling you assume the most effective fighting position.

Get up! Stop living in tomorrow, that place that kills your dreams. Tomorrow can only be achieved if you start doing things today.

Failure gives you the opportunity to propel yourself forward, but you must be the catapult. You have two options: stay on the ground, or take advantage of a firmer base from which to gain momentum.

I know that when I say it, it sounds damned easy to say. I know you'll say that this is all very easy for me to write from the comfort of my home. Well, yes, it is easy for me to say, because I'm an expert at falling down, and even more so at getting up. I am covered with scars from all the times I have fallen down, and I have come back smiling so many times that my smile begins to hurt.

Even I, who have had to get back up so many times, don't find it so easy. It is a difficult process, but it has made me increasingly stronger. I must admit that at times I have felt that God has abandoned me; with time I have come to understand that on many occasions He keeps silent so that we do not feel His shelter; this is what He did with Hezekiah: He made him believe that he was alone so that his heart would reveal all that was inside. But God did not do this so that He could discover what was in Hezekiah's heart, He did it so that Hezekiah could discover it for himself. The Lord withdraws so that you may search your heart; He moves back, but He never abandons you. Let's be brave and dare to look where we haven't looked for a long time.

Build with your words what you want to see tomorrow, build with deeds the promises of the *here and now*. No one can take your dreams from you, but they can take your ability to dream.

Get up, because from the ground everything looks daunting.

Throw yourself into the sea, because from the boat you can only feel the breeze, and not the power of the waves. If we desire and want to give direction to our lives, we have to exercise complete control over our faith. *Learned helplessness* is the term in psychology for beliefs that deprive us of our personal power, those that destroy our ability to react to what hurts us.

Depending on how you approach it, repetition can either make you a fool or a sage. Trying is not for the foolish, trying is for the brave. To those who are about to throw in the towel, who are waiting for the lethal blow, we must tell them that they need to try again, even if they think that it will be futile.

The key to the *feeling of failure* is to learn, adapt, and persevere. Learn as much from your falls as you can and absorb everything that they teach you. However, never allow yourself to fall apart. We must help others to understand that they cannot give up on themselves, because if they neglect their body, they will stop working, and if they neglect their spirit, everything will crumble inside.

Even with nothing, you can dream everything.

You don't need to travel to Tibet, or a monastic retreat to find yourself: just look in the mirror, there you are. You never went anywhere, you just refused to recognize yourself in that reflection and accept that it is you.

You have become distorted and confused, you have believed that you must look like that Instagram account, that celebrity, or you think that you must have those things in order for others to look up to you.

There is no answer lying behind the shamanic chants or Peyotism. The power that sustains the harmony of the universe pulsates within you. Be silent and listen carefully, bend your knees and take off your armor, lower your sword and touch the cold floor with your forehead. Don't be attached to anything, you are both nothing and everything.

Nothing enslaves you more than your contaminated emotions and thoughts. They lead you to believe in a reality that only exists in your head. Don't let money and ambition rob you of hope and joy.

Who the hell convinced you to beg? You are my blood; I am the coauthor of your book. It is time to open the eyes of the spirit and live as true heirs to the Kingdom. Fear not, for whatever you ask in faith will be given to you. Stand firm, don't give in and put a *maybe* where you had put a *no.*

Write down the new *maybes* in your life, and look deep into how you feel, what is your impression when you see a glimpse of the light?

Here is an example for you to follow:

~~Maybe~~   *I will forgive that person*

~~Maybe~~   *I will start that business*

~~Maybe~~   _____

~~Maybe~~   _____

~~Maybe~~   _____

~~Maybe~~   _____

~~Maybe~~   _____

The intention of placing a *maybe* on these actions is to stir your soul, cheat impossibility, and rekindle the flame of faith. If you can dare to hold on to this emotion and feed it, no matter how small and absurd it may seem to you, then you will be well on your way out of the stagnation and inertia of life.

The *maybe*s are a wonderful tool because they open the door of uncertainty. I love uncertainty, it tends to extract from me the best tools and gives a certain spice to life, one that only the expectation of the moment can provide. People worry about suggesting ideas because other people might think they are stupid. People are often judged by the risks they take because their reward will be proportionate to that risk. Make it worth the risk and not the pain.

Those who take risks inevitably find themselves destined to transform history in a positive way. The biggest mistake we make is to not try anything new.

The best creativity is the one that answers the question: "I'm not crazy, am I?" Paradoxical and absurd ideas are the catapult that propels you to the unimaginable, to true innovation in the present and toward a better future. We will discuss this in more detail later.

Only fools believe that there are dumb ideas.

There are no past or future mistakes, the only mistake is the mistake of not trying now. Don't measure your worth based on money, instead, focus on making the most of your time because once it's gone, you can't get it back. Quite often getting it right all the time can lead to a lack of fulfillment, I believe that getting it wrong is more fun when we try to create and innovate, to break trends and statistics.

Getting it right often closes you off from possibilities and keeps you from the mental growth that makes you hungry for more. We forget the infinite universe in front of us, which has not yet been navigated, and we end up staying on the shore watching others surf the waves of innovation: try to make a mistake by doing something new, mistakes make you believe more.

It is absurd to distrust creativity and be afraid of innovation, most of those who stick to the *status quo* are intensely afraid of change, because it threatens their traditions and rituals. Change is about getting rid of the old for the adventure of the new.

It is quite likely that we will find something wrong with the new, but it is a fact that the old way of doing things no longer works at the pace we are going. I suggest an amazing game of infinite possibilities, of imagining and conceiving new strategies to carry a message that impacts and transforms our already outdated way of seeing life, a new way of running companies, of doing business. Isn't it enthralling to imagine that there are things that no one else has thought of that you can create?

Chase it, like a dog chasing a hare. We shouldn't try to meet new challenges with old ideas and outdated tools, we will only end up frustrated.

We need to face risks head-on, even if we only make it halfway. Sooner or later, we will find the strength we need to achieve the goal and light the fuse, after spending so much time in the dark searching for it.

I always get excited when I think of my own plans; but when I think of God's plans, it ignites a different kind of fervor in me. The infinite is my end, there is no limit for me because eternity lies in my being.

Impossible is my favorite toy.

THE "SHOULD HAVE" EXISTS

Our mind usually creates connections between two types of logical structures: "This looks like that" or "this causes that". Based on these two processes, we are able to generate opinions, beliefs, and convictions that end up controlling and dominating our lives. This is where stereotypes come from, those cultural judgments that demonstrate the blindness of the mind and spirit. Let's transcend stereotypes, let's tear off the shackles of ignorance, let's do away with mediocrity, let's acquire the ability to listen, and let's abandon judgments, completely eliminating those judgments that we make carelessly.

Let's give ourselves the opportunity to see the big picture, from every angle, let's learn to walk in other people's shoes, let's swap hats, because sharing and changing ideas is progress.

Let's expand our ability to read the background, to overcome the obvious, to be prepared for the unknown. Can't you see that the world is too vast and your feet are too small to stay in one place all your life?

I know it's tempting to have so many possibilities ahead of you, but believe me, it's even more exciting to watch the exhilaration of the uncertainty of not being sure of anything. Don't be afraid to talk to others, to get to know them. We speak the same language, but we sound different even when we say the same thing. No matter how difficult, distant, or complicated it may seem, the only way to reach the summit of your dreams is to conquer it with your feet.

I need the journey like the addict needs his fix, I know that sooner or later I will need to up the dosage, and I hope you do too. Many cling to what they call home, and dare not leave it for the supposed warmth or security it provides. You are the only one who can transform a cave into a room for two and a room for two into your true home.

If you dream of starting a business you need to prepare yourself for a journey, a real adventure, not a vacation.

I want to remind you that *the "should have" exists*, and that it exists to torment you, we will see later on that this is indeed what it does. The worst thing you could do right now is to stay in your chair dreaming, pining for something that will never happen. Until you put your feet to the asphalt and start sweating, there is no way that you can turn what you want into a reality. You don't get to feel the cold of the mountains by looking at a map.

Break down the stereotypes in your mind, and get moving. Travel, trek, conquer. Live and see what's beyond.

Capisci?

Chapter 5

Grab the train

Watching someone else totally go for it can be incredibly upsetting to the person who's spent a lifetime building a case for why they themselves can't.

Jen Sincero

O nce you help someone get back on their feet, you then need to get them back on the path that will lead them to being unbreakable, showing them the opportunities that lay ahead; taking advantage of those opportunities is the best way to get rid of the *feeling of failure*.

There is no such thing as the perfect moment, that's a lie, an illusion entrenched in time, in uncertainties and anxieties. There are opportunities that will only come along once in your life, they are unique and exclusive to you. When that happens, things will no longer be as they were before. You let those opportunities go, you saw them, but you didn't protect them; maybe they come with secrets that can only be uncovered with wisdom, taken not only once we are ready but also when we are eager.

It is more important in life to be willing than to be prepared.

❁

Go for it, slowly but surely, go for it. Keep on running until you reach the finish line exhausted, screaming, in pain, bruised, and injured, but unbreakable.

Shout it to the mountains and to the beaches: "I took chances, I confronted my fears, I made progress, I took on challenges, I had dreams, I imagined this life, I soared and I stumbled."

Go for it! Nothing can stop anyone who doesn't give up, and if you are overcome with fear at any point along the way, you know you are on the right track. Fear is the sign that everything will pay off. As I said, facing small amounts of fear in life can help you build resilience, you must not let fear consume you or hold you back, use it as motivation to face challenges head-on, like a fearless warrior in battle.

One day your wounds will be healed and you will receive the crown worthy of your faith. Now you have seen what lies ahead in your future, it's time to make those plans a reality. The rest will fall into place.

Nothing will come unless you actively search for it and make the effort to attain it yourself. Some people expect prosperity, financial stability, and employment, believing that all they have to do is pray. But prayer is not just about asking, it is also a tool that gives us the

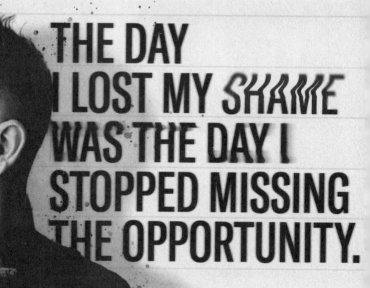

THE DAY
I LOST MY *SHAME*
WAS THE DAY I
STOPPED MISSING
THE OPPORTUNITY.

courage and determination that we need to be able go after what we want for ourselves.

Prayer alone is not enough: first we have to ask, then we have to seek, and then we have to make things happen.

We treat life like a Polaroid camera, we want everything right away, and our desire for immediate results is reflected in how we pray. Often, kneeling to pray brings us immediate results, but on other occasions it does not. The only thing we can know for sure is that prayer is the most powerful weapon in the universe, and that the prayers of a faithful son will always be heard.

When it comes to learning to pray, there's nothing like a bit of turbulence.

We have to look for opportunities, we can't expect doors to open for us if we don't actively take the initiative to knock on them. Taking only one step is not enough to get the results you've been waiting for.

Opportunities are like a train, they usually come along early in the morning, that's right, when you are still sleeping, because you think that this is your time to rest. This train flies by so quickly, it usually doesn't even make any stops.

Almost everyone sees it fly by, but they don't get on it. They get on board, because that requires buying a ticket. We want opportunity without having to pay the price. Conversely, the unbreakable get on that train whether they are ready for it or not; as soon as they see that opportunity, they grab it, they don't just watch the carriages fly past them, they don't hesitate: "Shall I get on", "shall I not get on", they don't even stop to ask: "will it be okay?", "will it turn out well?", "will I feel comfortable?", will this be the train I've always hoped for?" Absolutely not! The unbreakable refuse to allow negative thoughts to get in their way: they hear it coming from miles away, they prepare themselves, they work hard, assess the situation, calculate distance and speed, and when it finally approaches, they face it head-on without hesitation: BAM! They get on board.

And what about the people already on the train, how do they react? Well, they immediately resort to attacking them with punches and kicks, while also showering them with insults and negative comments. But the unbreakable don't give a damn what anyone says, they are not bothered by mockery or ridicule when it comes to facing their destiny, because they have always worked hard; they simply show their determination, reveal their strength, cling to the iron of the carriage, and once they are on that train, they transform it and start getting things done.

The reason the unbreakable don't care about these things is that they know that the love of their life, or the investors they need to meet, could be traveling on that train. They don't know whether they will end up laying the cornerstones of the company they dreamed of, or whether that new job, new house, or family they have always wanted will be on board that train. They don't know, they just got on board, no matter what their parents, partner, cousin, or neighbor said; they didn't pay attention to those who said they wouldn't make it. And there they are, scuffed, sweaty, scarred, and bloody, but on board.

All the people who were on board, dressed in suits and ties, turn to look at them, and they just smile and say to them: "I'm on the train, I don't care what anyone says, It doesn't matter what I was thinking before I got on, what matters is that I'm here now."

When they see the train pulling away, the people left on the platform realize that this was their train, and when they see the last carriage fade into the distance, they say: "That was my train." These are the type of people that think that the *should have doesn't exist*, but it does exist, as we have reflected on in the previous chapter. It is a ghostly presence that appears to haunt you throughout your life. A ghost that will haunt you when you are 35, 45, 55 years old, when you are in the comfort of your home it will say: "What would have happened if...?", "What would have been if...?"; it will be there when you talk to your grandchildren and tell them: "I almost made it", "I was going to be a great soccer player", "I had the potential to be the best singer", "I was almost a great architect", "I could have been the most distinguished poet", "I could have been the most outstanding astronomer", "I could have become the most accomplished mathematician", "I almost made it to the moon, I almost did, but when my train came, I hesitated and never got on".

That ghost will haunt you until the day you decide to get on the next train, otherwise it may be the one that is recorded on your tombstone: "Here lies Mr. *Almost*", or "Mrs. *Could Have Been*". Life belongs to those who persevere, to those who do not give up, to those who dare. Stop being an *almost*.

All of them say to themselves: "When I raise a million, I will start my first business", "when I pay off the car I will have my first child", "when I complete my doctorate and triple master's degree I will write a book", they should know that the opportunity is slipping away from them, because while they are preparing, someone else will snatch it away from them.

The unbreakable know what they have to do and what they need to achieve their goals, they understand that their arsenal consists of much more than economic or material resources, that their strength lies in the power of their emotions and attitudes. They rely on their natural adrenaline that the body gives them, and they use it to push forward; they know that there is nothing stronger than the constancy, firmness, and greatness of their spirit.

They are not blinded by talents, money, status, or power, they do not see themselves like the losers with PhDs, or like the people who are rich but miserable.

If you wait for the perfect moment, it will be gone by the time you realize it was there.

I want to make sure that people don't miss out on opportunities because they think they don't have enough resources. Pick three goals you have yet to achieve, then feel free to repeat the exercise with more goals if you like.

In the first column, write your wishes.

In the second column, using a different color, write down what it is that you need to move forward. Here you should focus on specific resources, such as a loan, a partner, a house with a bigger bedroom, or machinery.

In the third column, and again with a different color, list your intangible assets, things that you must develop within yourself, such as discipline, tolerance to criticism, or frugality.

Once you have done the exercise, I need you to answer, whether if you had all the items listed in the second column, but not those in the third column, would you still be able to achieve your goals?

Would you be able to succeed with the money, but without the discipline? Would your business advance if you get the premises, but you fail to overcome the fear of networking with others? Would you finish your project if the bank gives you the credit, but you don't kick the habit of putting off tasks for later? If your answer is "no", you will

What do you want?	What material or financial resources do you need?	What skills and strengths should you develop?
•	•	•
•	•	•
•	•	•
•	•	•
•	•	•
•	•	•
•	•	•
•	•	•
•	•	•
•	•	•
•	•	•
•	•	•
•	•	•
•	•	•
•	•	•
•	•	•
•	•	•

see that you need to do away with the excuses that keep you from moving forward: the problem is you.

Let go of what's holding you back the most: you.

This does not mean that you will be able to achieve your desires without material resources, it will be difficult, but without the personal qualities that come from you, success will be unattainable.

The restrictions you face often become entangled with each other. If you address one, you will notice that the others start to loosen up. Willpower is like a muscle, it requires exercise but it also gets exhausted. The more we reinforce it, the more plasticity it develops and the better it forms to the shape of the mold we want for our life. In the same way as when we begin to exercise our body, it becomes easier for us to subdue our cravings and temptations, when we begin to uproot the vices that keep us from our vision, we develop greater discipline and it becomes easier to move forward.

Once you start on your way, you will obtain the material resources you need to carry on.

Self-control is the ability to subdue our emotions and not let them control us, or prevent us from being able to decide what we want to feel at any given moment.

Our reluctance to take risks and pursue new opportunities stems from our innate aversion to conflict. We avoid at all costs situations where we might experience pain.

Start by facing up to your fears, don't look for an absolute victory, try to take small steps, even if you are afraid, do it nonetheless.

It only takes one small act of courage in your life to step out of the hole you're in and fully embrace your dreams: Take the leap now!

91

Courageous people are not those who don't feel afraid, but those who, in spite of their fear, go on the offensive. Our minds naturally seek calm and tend to take the path of least resistance, often steering clear of risks at any cost.

The unbreakable must oppose this natural tendency that induces us to lie back on the couch while the train passes right in front of our door. I have always been willing to taking risks, I never seek assurances, I would rather fail than to think that I might have missed out on any moment in life. I continue moving forward, even if that means enduring great injury as I go on my way.

Those of you who are coauthoring this book with me, and who already know that the obstacles are within us, should now take on the role of ticket seller so that everyone can get on the next train.

IF YOU KEEP LOOKING AT THE CLOCK,
YOU WILL ALWAYS BE LATE FOR LIFE.

NOT TODAY, NOT EVER

Let's make it clear once and for all, we are not the victims, in fact, I believe that we are more like the suspects in the crime. We have killed more dreams and virtues than the challenges and sufferings that we have faced in our own life. Stop blaming others for your failures and take responsibility once and for all.

And when you do, you'll have to overcome who you are until your own limits are broken down. But it will take time: learning to do things the right way doesn't happen overnight. It is important to be patient and strive for excellence in order to experience ongoing improvement.

It takes many hours of training and an iron discipline to learn to build, to lead, to be firm in our convictions, to not give up in the face of adversity, which at times is exhausting and absurdly demanding. I owe this to my mother who not only taught me recipes for the kitchen, but also showed me the ingredients for life. I owe it to my wife who has always encouraged me never to stop, but to keep getting better. I owe it to you and to those who have trusted in my words, to everyone who shares my message, and even to those who challenge me and disagree with my content.

It took me a long time to learn to examine things thoroughly, to study diligently, to seek the truth with a razor-sharp focus, to be faithful to my calling, to put my thoughts in order, and to focus my passion and courage. It wasn't easy to clear the cobwebs from my mind and commit to daily tasks, but that didn't stop me from throwing myself at the opportunities that came my way.

I cleared my heart and mind from unhealthy images and thoughts, and I purified the emotions and intentions behind my actions. It took a great deal of effort to pull myself together and embrace hundreds of thousands of people, to strengthen my spirit.

Life is not about pretending to be perfect, it is about challenging yourself to push the boundaries of your mental and spiritual capabilities, to break free from your comfort zone and reach new heights that you never thought possible. When they try to put you in their mold, break it!

The challenge lies not in the summit itself, but in getting there, appreciating the view without becoming too attached, avoiding being influenced by the surroundings, coming back down, down even further, and after reaching the bottom, making the journey back up, but this time bringing someone else with you.

Our job is to get everyone to surpass everything that they believe to be insurmountable, to have the energy, the grit, and the tenacity. We should be individuals who walk, run, and fly without getting weary, like the royal swift. When a chance presents itself to you, go ahead and kiss her on the lips, even if she responds with a slap.

Don't be afraid of the result, because our life is about the process. I don't understand this obsession with the end, when really the only thing that matters is the journey, as if the only thing that has value in a book is the last page.

Your life is not finished yet: even if the world has tried to end it, it will be God that determines its end.

Chapter 6

Deadly distractions

When I'm in my coffin with my hands tied
together and a cloth wrapped around
my head to keep my mouth from falling
open, that's when I'll resign myself.
Federico García-Lorca

One of the reasons why we find it so hard to get on board the train of opportunity is because we all have unfinished business. There are extraordinarily bright people who fail to achieve their goals. When we are asked how these things can happen, we are faced with several factors, including attitude problems, low self-esteem, lack of purpose, or lack of willpower. These illnesses share a common symptom: leaving everything until later.

Procrastination often results from a lack of willpower and failure to effectively use fear, which, as we will soon see, can be a powerful motivational tool when we know how to manage it.

Getting started with what we need to do is vital when it comes to being unbreakable. Avoiding distractions significantly impacts our results. Many people sit down to work and within minutes they are on their phones, scrolling through Instagram images or looking at a recipe they found in an old magazine. These small distractions are lethal.

How many times have you said: "I'll do it on Monday", "when this movie's finished, I'll get started...", "I'll play one more game and then...?" And you don't do it that Monday or the next, and you watch that movie and then another one, which you've already seen, and you move the time forward on the tablet so you can play another game.

When motivation dies, discipline resurrects it.

Procrastination is rooted in a sense of comfort, because getting things done generates results, and this propels you forward.

Deep down, you have convinced yourself into believing that you are shielded under armor that protects you from uncertainty and the decisions that need to be made. However, this is not the case, you need to move away from the primitive part of your brain that believes doing nothing keeps you safe, because inaction is like a ticking time bomb of uncertainties. Taking control of your life through your actions is not the same as surrendering control through what you let go. Venturing out of the cave to gather berries comes with the risk of encountering predators, but it is a known risk that you take in order to

Don¹   [dän]

From the latin **donum**

1. m. Dávida, present or gift.

2. m. Special grace, quality or the ability to do something.
U.t. in *sent. irón.*

3. m. Rel. Natural or supernatural good Christians have, with respect
to God, from the one who receives it.

Giving less than you can,

is to sacrifice a

GIFT.

achieve your goal. I've got some bad news for you, buddy: you have to leave the cave or you'll starve to death. If you delay, when you eventually leave the cave, it will not be on your own terms, the conditions will be imposed on you by the relentless sands of time that do not stop falling.

Many results can come from taking action, but only defeat comes from inertia.

I am tired of seeing brilliant ideas that, because they were left to the last minute, become a crude imitation of what they were intended to be. When you postpone the essential steps for consolidating your projects, you may not think you have decided how you will live the next few years, but you are mistaken: that is exactly what you have done. Not taking action is the most impactful decision a person can make, because time stops for nobody.

Wishes and intentions are all useless without the power of action. Being interested and being committed are two very different things. The verbs *to want*, *to dream*, and *to desire* must be used in a more limited way, and the verbs *to do*, *to fight*, and *to endeavor* must be used more often. We have to put the verbs in order: link the past of *desire* with the present of *act* to obtain the future of *succeed*.

Today, use your time to work hard, use your talents and gifts to serve, and use your money to invest in yourself and in your growth. When have you ever seen anything good come out of idleness, or anything great come out of passivity, or love and peace come out of resentment? When have you ever seen abundance grow out of laziness?

There are some things that don't require *money*: being passionate, having ethics, being punctual, and making a start to doing something. Use this to your advantage and everything else will fall into place. However small and meager you may consider your talents and gifts, they will be enough to achieve success if you focus them on the objective.

Dreams are not achieved through laziness, indifference, apathy, procrastination, "I can't", "I'll do it tomorrow", "if only I could..." None of that! Stop putting up with your mental inertia and stop with the excuses and procrastination. You need a desire that is so deep that no matter how much you are beaten and humiliated, you will always get back up. You need strength, but above all constancy.

Everything is impossible for lazy minds.

Procrastination is a bad habit, it is a vice that not only hinders your progress, but also comes at a great, great financial cost, you'll see. Few vices can be overcome without help. Support others and be there to help those who need to start putting emphases on the right vowels.

Kicking a bad habit is a win, but sometimes we see having to change behaviors as a loss, and no one likes the feeling of losing. The truth is that those who lose the most are those who are the most resistant to change.

It is an unfortunate paradox that procrastination is so common among brilliant minds and highly creative people who fail to channel the power of their genius. Another type of procrastination comes in the form of perfectionism and manifests in individuals who, hiding behind their perfectionism, end up failing to accomplish anything.

Procrastination is not only a matter of putting things off until later, it also consists of all the evasive actions that we take at an unconscious level in order to avoid doing the things that matter most. This includes delay, perfectionism, over-analysis, and indecision; the latter frequently occurs as a way of avoiding confronting the empty page or making that all-important phone call.

If we keep focusing all of our mind and spirit on what we don't want, we will continue to get the same outcome.

We are not talking about putting off tedious tasks like cleaning or taking out the trash, which, although we hate doing them, we prefer, if it means avoiding what we should really be doing, those tasks that have a decisive impact on our lives.

Simple tasks that take us weeks to start or that we don't get around to starting at all. Basic tasks such as updating a CV or drawing up a plan for a personal project get buried under the overwhelming weight of TV series, video games, WhatsApp groups, and never-ending memes.

This doesn't mean that you should work without taking a break. Enjoying some entertainment is an important part of achieving the plans that you have set out for yourself. However, you must be conscious of where you place leisure time on your list of priorities. If you go about it in a smart way, you'll enjoy those breaks much more, because you'll know that you're in control of your life.

Another factor that leads us to postpone our basic tasks is the poor establishment of priorities. I know you've heard it said many times before, that there are important issues and there are urgent issues, and that our focus should be on the former, but this is something you must never forget. We should also keep in mind that this will always be a subjective decision, and will inevitably be influenced by our personal biases and prejudices. Even if we have a well-organized system in place to prioritize what is important and urgent, it is ultimately our actions that will determine our success.

Complete the exercise, do it thoroughly, because we will revisit it in a few chapters.

I want you to make a list of the five things that are most important to you right now, things that you need to accomplish such as drawing up a budget or sitting down to study a subject that you need to learn about. Next to it, I want you to write down a date by which you can reasonably accomplish the task.

Then, over the course of a few days, document your activities; meticulously record the time spent on social media, unless it's part of your personal project, watching TV, or writing text messages, as well as any other potential distractions that get in the way of your work. If you want, feel free to remove from the list the time you allocate specifically for taking care of your body and rejuvenating your mind.

It is also important that you keep track of the distractions that may occur when undertaking a task. How many times do you stop working to do something that isn't very important, how many times do you check your phone or stop working without having made any progress?

Five key tasks	Minutes of distraction	Work interruptions

This review will give you an idea of what the escape routes are. Make no mistake, sometimes household chores are the perfect excuse to get out of the chair, you must identify when cutting some onions is due to hunger or just a mere distraction. We may also take false solace in doing tasks that we think are productive when they are not, such as answering pointless emails or attending endless meetings. This exercise will also help you to establish an optimal place to work, if you don't already have one.

All jobs require a place that is as free from distractions as possible, but our workplace won't do anything for us unless we exercise discipline. In today's world, smartphones are the biggest distraction of all. Turn it off, and put a lid on that constant chatterbox. If for whatever reason you can't do that, you can at least limit its power to distract you: turn off notifications, place it well out of reach, ask your most important contacts to refrain from sending you unnecessary messages.

Once you know which distractions interrupt your work the most, you can keep them at bay. Don't start working without having the necessary material, and don't use it for anything other than work.

When you feel you have made progress in doing this, you will be able to progress further. Practicing serenity reinforces self-control. If you are someone who travels frequently or lacks control over your environment, you can enhance your focus by intentionally exposing yourself to challenging situations that can test your patience and break your concentration.

Later usually turns into never.

During my exercise routine, there is a technique that I use, every alternating day, to enhance my focus: I listen to a continuous audio stream, or something loud, for 10 minutes, which causes discomfort and disrupts my peace; in doing this, my aim is to concentrate so intensely that I am able to block out all external noises. At times, I am able to block out all external noises and disturbances, almost like having a mental filter, which helps me control what information I let in from the outside world when I want to focus on a task. Practicing this exercise will help you learn to turn up the volume on your inner thoughts and ignore the distractions that your mind throws at you. Practice being in tune and identify the things you need to let go and eliminate from your heart.

Prayer (or meditation, if you are not a believer) is a great help, because through prayer you find a space in which to know yourself better, and the more you know yourself, the less afraid you become.

The most effective way of protecting yourself from temptation is to keep yourself occupied with good. When our thoughts consistently flow in an upward direction, they become deep and steadfast, they are held free of any deviations or distractions; then, the imagination and the feelings that spring from the depths of the soul are naturally directed forward. This is the undisputed path to excellence. If you want a better existence, you need to be better, it's as simple as that. Nothing gets better if you don't get better first.

Few people take the trouble to write down their goals and dreams with finely tuned clarity. Draw up a plan and a strategy, apply it and forget about the famous plan B: you have to get there no matter what.

Use your time wisely, let go of the things that distract you and learn to say no: "I'm not going", "I don't want to", "I can't". Don't spend your time on anything that doesn't bring you closer to your life purpose, which will also serve to elevate others. Don't put your comforts before your needs.

If you have allocated three hours at the computer, make sure you stay there for the entire duration. At first you will feel like you are wasting your time, but then you will see that these are the moments that produce the most productivity. And if you don't know where to start, start at the end, or in the middle, but at least start. You will learn to connect the pieces, and once you do, it will feel like you were the missing piece all along.

YOU DON'T NEED MORE

HOURS IN THE DAY'

You need
Priorities.

THE PRICE OF BEING DIFFERENT

Are you going to carry on lounging around on the sofa? Are you going to spend 40 years like this?

Have you ever thought about how short our time is here on earth?

Let's suppose you are happy with what you have now: you feel peace and joy. If you still have a strong desire to grow, why are you hesitating to go out and conquer the world?

Every time you declare yourself to be well, you are stating your own demise. And especially if you know that there are still things you need to do, strategies you can use, and joys you can experience.

I ask you again: What the hell are you waiting for?

Write it down here, so I know:

- ☐ The perfect time

- ☐ The million dollars

- ☐ The dream partner

- ☐ The stray headhunter

- ☐ The university degree

- ☐ Social approval

- ☐ A sign from heaven

- ☐ Angelic epiphany

You are terrified to do what your heart desires. The way we use resources in this world matters much more than how much we use them; how much you do matters much more than how much you know. We have already mentioned that being ready comes before being prepared. You can have all the knowledge in the world, but it will not do you any good unless you have the willingness to focus and get things done every day.

Procrastination is a form of self-sabotage, by which we avoid the tasks we need to do instead of facing them head-on. This is evident in the excuses you invent to delay a tomorrow that never comes.

Let go of what you don't need to carry; it's not that you lack time, it's that you waste the time you have. Don't confuse being too busy with being too productive, and be mindful of these small cracks in your life, as these small flaws can lead to significant setbacks.

Don't focus on starting, focus on finishing. Few things are more rewarding than completing a necessary task, regardless of the scale of progress made toward achieving our goals.

Get a new dose of inspiration. Stress does not come from thinking about what we have not started, but rather from the anxiety induced by the looming pressure to complete them.

If you want victory, you have to be prepared to go to war; you have to enter the battle, to fully commit to the cause, risk injury, and face the possibility of losing comrades in the process. Unless you think that life is just a *picnic*?

You will often have to say "yes" to things that scare you, but this is the only way to know if "*you have what it takes* to be successful". Do this from time to time and you will see that these challenges are there to push you out of your comfort zone and help you to grow.

Even if your initial attempt seems feeble, you have to demonstrate your strength immediately. We all need some ferocity; in this jungle you either roar or you stay a sheep forever.

Believing in your abilities means nothing if you don't use them.

If you don't do it, nobody will believe in you. Understand that this is the price of being different. It may be a high price, but it is the cost of human dignity.

It is better to be a crazy entrepreneur than a sane and bitter employee. Stop handing out résumés and start handing out flyers for your own business.

When you do things, do them with love, with passion, with wisdom, with vision, with focus, without fear, and without looking back. And be prepared: there is no better investment than the investment into your own knowledge. Study, understand, and focus, be sure to discern every word and every subject. Apply what you have learned, knowledge held captive in your mind is like a book that is never opened.

Every moment in your life should be savored as a chance to learn. Don't let a day go by that you can do without, a day that you say: "I could have lived without today."

That would be truly catastrophic.

Chapter 7

Just let your legs tremble

*My most fearful steps have been
the most dignified of my life.*

Anyha Ruiz

We have already said that procrastination is often the result of the poor management of fear. Not having enough fear, as well as having too much of it, leads to paralysis and inaction.

Fear is a reaction that often results in self-sabotage. It is buried so deeply in our spirit that we sweep it under the rug and forget that it's there; then we start believing that we just aren't cut out to succeed.

When you face fear head-on, when you choose to no longer see it as a barrier, but instead dismantle the obstacle it creates in order to overcome it, you can use it as motivation to reach your goals, that is when you will discover that what scared you was far worse in your imagination than in reality. Don't fall into mind games or anticipate defeat.

Fear is a deceitful companion, a comrade that exaggerates everything out of proportion. We are the ones who dictate the role it must fulfill in our life; it can be the barrier that prevents us from moving forward or the fuel from which we draw the energy to continue. Without it, our species would have

The mind is more chaotic than reality.

been nothing more than food for predators; without our power to overcome fear, we would still be hiding in caves. Today, many people who do not manage to overcome fear dwell in the deepest of darkness: mediocrity, that void of "if only there had been..."

Fear of success is due to neuro-narrative associations that lead to repetitive behaviors. Our life is dominated by opinions, beliefs, and convictions; it is driven by two great engines: pleasure and pain. Of course, our opinions can be diluted; but to destroy an opinion, we must first plant the seeds of doubt, and certainly, to destroy a belief, we must first question it. Convictions and beliefs are not the same, the latter can change, while the former are those certainties for which we are willing to die.

The unbreakable are afraid because they pursue immensity, they impose challenges on themselves that are frightening even just to

Aren't you more afraid of being told "YES" than of being told "NO"?

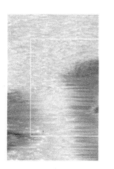  

imagine. Greatness, glory, and success are only idyllic and peaceful states when we fantasize about them, but when we conceive them with the intention of carrying them out, of making them a reality, they generate fear.

The legs of the unbreakable tremble when they stand up to challenges, but they remain steadfast and calm when it comes to overcoming their greatest fears. There will always be a goal, a reason that stirs excitement in our hearts, a new opportunity to progress.

Fear does not overcome, it is used to overcome.

Maybe you heard *no* so many times in the past that you eventually ended up being a realist. How many times have you thought you were better off before you tried doing something? Of course, uncertainty generates fear, but certainty is a direct route to mediocrity. We think that we will achieve these successes on our own, but we won't: whoever goes first, leads the way. He who takes the lead provides the tools to make success a reality, so we must be willing to apply these tools as weapons.

Fear is rooted in a fallacy, in the absence of faith. Fear will fill you with excuses to justify yourself, but all that comes from fear is more fear:

1) Fear of not being worthy of success.
2) Fear of not being able to meet expectations.
3) Fear of not being able to face the commitments involved in starting a personal project.
4) Fear of being rejected.
5) Fear of losing everyday comforts.

6) Fear of saying "no" to certain delights or people.

Get rid of limiting thoughts. Fear of success is characterized by several behaviors that would require an entire chapter to explain, but I will highlight a few that I consider to be essential:

If you mismanage your fear of success, you are likely to exhibit one or more of the following behaviors:

I cannot stop negative thoughts from entering my mind, but I can stop them from remaining there.

1) You are underperforming.
2) You focus on those who reject you and not on those who accept you.
3) You lose focus of your objective.
4) You think others deserve success, but not you.
5) Procrastination.
6) You shy away from suffering.
7) You have an overwhelming aversion to conflict.

I want to focus on the last of these aspects. Every day, we are confronted with a range of conflicts, which vary in intensity and present themselves in diverse forms and contexts. Certainly, there are differences in personality and upbringing that lead us to deal with conflict in different ways. Even so, we can modify how we approach it.

From an early age, we are forced to make decisions and face up to numerous conflicts. Our humanity renders us vulnerable to the challenges and consequences of these conflicts, yet the renowned figures of history have all been shaped through enduring the ruthless

A person's true nature is better understood by their reactions than by their actions.

❀

impact of adversity: David, Paul, Ruth, Alexander the Great, Joan of Arc, Churchill, Marie Curie, Mandela, Martin Luther King, Gandhi, to mention a few, all went through moments of enormous crisis that brought to the surface their concern, stress, or anxiety, typical of human beings.

We experience internal, interpersonal, marital, relational, work, social, community, national, and global conflicts. These instances arise when multiple values, perspectives, or opinions clash, rendering it impossible to reconcile them. These contradictions are typically superficial, and it is we who render them irreconcilable.

We must first acknowledge that at times we become so engulfed in our problems that we are unable to find a solution, even when it is within reach. Sometimes there isn't even a conflict per se.

But how should we react to a conflict? When we manage our emotions while taking action, we are in control. On the other hand, when we only react, we get conflict.

We need to understand how to manage and ultimately master our emotions in order to prevent them from clouding our judgment and disrupting our sense of balance.

Turn down the volume on fear and you will hear what God wants to tell you.

❀

Here comes the key question: How do we master our emotions? Emotions originate from a basic and abstract world, but by placing them in a neutral context and examining them before assigning them a name, we can achieve some small success. In this way we will

116

ensure that they do not turn into polluted feelings. This is a complex exercise, but with daily practice and mindful effort, you can improve your skills by using as a starting point the action that triggered the emotion.

Self-control is the ability that allows us to subdue our emotions and not fall into their clutches. This gives us the possibility to choose what we want to feel in any given moment of our life. Human beings tend to turn their backs on conflicts. We steer clear of circumstances that may lead to suffering, and this in turn leads to procrastination.

In its search for peace, the mind chooses the path of least resistance, it avoids dealing with insecurities at all costs. At times, our frustration arises from not having the necessary tools to handle a situation, leading us to feel the need to express our emotions in order to feel like we are doing something.

Not everything you confront can be changed, but nothing you don't confront will change. Sometimes you will have to wage war on the false peace that you have created in your mind, in order to finally achieve an enduring peace, rather than settling for superficial tranquility.

We lose a lot more through fear than courage, much more is lost when we choose to retreat rather than take a chance. Whoever takes the least risk, loses the most. We often think that our city or neighborhood is too small for the business we dream of and we stop in our tracks out of fear. When someone else takes a risk that we were unwilling to take, we realize that what was lost is greater than what we are left with.

Feed your dreams so much that your fears starve.

117

Without fear there is no greatness, no great feats can be achieved if we don't live in a constant state of self-improvement. This doesn't mean that you have to create a situation of permanent stress, if you do, you will end up getting sick. But a prudent dose of stress allows us to get out of bed, it is the cup of coffee that wakes up our soul, so that it can then be nourished by prayer. The unbreakable seek success, but do not settle for it, because they know that when they push forward many others follow in their footsteps, they try because they are the beacons that mark the way and protect their territory like watchtowers.

The unbreakable do not lend their ears to opinions that seek to discourage them, nor to temptations of vanity; they are courageous because they nourish their inner self, even if fools believe that their brilliance lies only on the outside. The intensity that burns on the inside shines through on the outside.

We must use fear to our advantage. It may be simple to put into writing, but putting it into action requires courage and determination. Using fear to our advantage is only possible when we integrate it into our daily lives. When we first learn to drive, we are terrified at the thought of taking the fast lane, but gradually we make small advances until we are able to drive on the highway with the steering wheel in one hand and a coffee in the other.

Put a muzzle on that *dog*.

This is what happens when fear becomes a normal part of our daily lives and no longer terrifies us. Over time, we forget the specific moment when we no longer felt fear.

As we conquer minor fears, it becomes easier to overcome greater ones: talking to new people, entrepreneurship, applying for a job, boarding a plane, or challenging the *status quo* are all situations that you can subdue gradually by making modest advances. Trust in your inner spirit will give you the resilience needed to overcome fear and develop boldness.

There is one exercise that I suggest you do in your own personal writings, rather than on these pages. Think of a situation, person, or thing that evokes fear for you in your life. It could be, for example, public speaking or watching horror movies; in that case, create a plan to start overcoming that fear. Begin by taking small actions, starting with the easiest tasks and gradually progressing to a level that you currently feel is unthinkable. Keep a record of your progress, indicate the date on which you faced the challenges and write down how you felt before and after.

Your progress will be defined by the nature of the fear you face and your ability to overcome it. Once you have overcome the fear that today is holding you back, make sure to share your story on social media using the hashtags #OvercomingFear #Unbreakables. You can include a short text and tell other unbreakable people about your process, from the children's merry-go-round to the roller coaster that makes you feel dizzy just looking at it.

How can anyone lead others when they don't have the means to lead themselves?

Once you have discovered and overcome the cause of your fear, you must keep on persevering, being responsible, consistent, diligent, and, last but not least, you must enjoy the satisfaction of having succeeded.

Even if you are terrified now, you need to enhance your ability to cope with life's challenges, to transform pain into a driving force so that you can overcome trials and use them to make you stronger.

FEAR KILLS

At some point in our lives, we have all wanted to be someone we are not; either out of admiration or to satisfy our own expectations. In those moments we have doubts and live in denial of our identity, we set aside all the inherent traits and qualities we were born with. If you struggle with emotional hiccups, like a frivolous celebrity or a puppet without a sense of self, I want to tell you that you have become an imitated version of others, you have lost all your originality.

You still have time to break free from social expectations and the taming of your dreams, if you've been stifled by your idiosyncrasies, it's time to embrace that uniqueness that others may have discouraged you from expressing.

Everyone in life has a disruptive, rebellious, wild, countercultural and deranged side. If you have hidden your individuality beneath feelings of frustration, in response to criticisms that have left you mute behind a facade of conformity, you must remember that the unconventional you could change the world if given the chance to flourish. You could be running an entire country and helping millions of people, but no, you've got it held captive. Do you know why? Because you believed the bunch of mediocre people who couldn't make it and made sure you didn't either.

You were made to soar, but you stayed on the ground, listening to those who crawl.

122

They changed your innate factory settings. And it all started when you were labeled as "foolish", "romantic", "fanciful", "deluded", and when you faced criticism from those who were not able to do anything themselves, you allowed yourself to be swayed, and you retreated to a state of stagnation. This world needs more *dreamers* and fewer *realists:* more creative and innovative, less judgmental and envious.

Don't tell me that you have no regrets about something you didn't say out of fear or shame, about keeping silent when you should have spoken out, about stalling when you should have taken action. Don't tell me you don't regret not having cried more, not having kissed more, not having laughed more. I know that today you say that you risked doing something crazy for that person. I also know that you are going to say: "Look, Daniel, I'm already (put your age here), and I'm too old for this. I can't go around doing crazy things. I don't have time to dream anymore."

Well, dreaming is what keeps you young, and although your body may have aged, if you stop dreaming, your mind and heart will grow old too.

In this life you have to be more like a child, to have a tender heart, as God tells us. This will mean that our hearts will become huge. It's perfectly acceptable to be mature in terms of biological age, but don't lose the ability to be amazed at what you can accomplish.

With a single toy, a child can win the most brutal of battles, fly across the universe with a bag as a cape, and forgive without a second thought. Why don't you do the same right now?

I'll tell you why: because you're afraid of being called idealistic, weak, or naive.

Stop caring what they say, the world is not about good people, or perfect people, or the right people. This game is about people who have shortcomings and limitations, like you and me, but who decided to change their prognosis because they broadened their minds and deepened their hearts.

The world is about people who are effective, hungry to achieve, to get, to give, to serve, to love, and to conquer, but above all to colonize, because there is no point in conquering without colonizing.

Have they ever called you childish? Well, don't stop feeling like a child.

Have they ever called you hungry? Well, don't stop satisfying your appetite.

Have they ever called you crazy? So, don't stop trying.

Chapter 8

Don't sleep much at all

My actions are the manifestations of my prayers.

Elena Brower

When you start doing the things that you have to get done, and you lose the fear of success, of what people will say and of the changes that your new life will bring, you will see that there will be no stopping you. At that moment, the bell will ring, and the most important battle will begin, a battle in which you must conquer yourself.

At that moment, you will engage in a battle with the fiercest opponent you have ever faced, and overcoming it will bring you the greatest satisfaction, although every blow you deal will hurt you in equal measure.

We urgently need a mind trained to withstand and tolerate conflict. When I was younger, I had the opportunity to know extremely smart people; some of my classmates were extremely gifted; they all had master's degrees or doctorates, they were the kind of people who had vast memories; whereas when I was a child, I could barely remember the capital of a state. I was always less suited to the demands of school, and less adapted to the demands imposed by society. That (relative) disadvantage made me more tenacious, it forced me to work three times as much as those who made it without much effort, which served as a great blessing.

Where it only took some people a single step, it would take me a whole marathon; I had to be so determined in order to succeed, it was like smashing through the windows of heaven. My ammunition was discipline, obedience, and perseverance. I never gave up and I never will. Those who know me know the storms I have had to weather.

He who does not control the river of his thoughts ends up drowning in a sea of emotions.

Those who didn't make it were those who lacked interest, and those of us who did make it, did so because we were committed to winning the battle against ourselves. I ask God without hesitation, He never tires of giving, and I never tire of asking. When you ask for little, you get little, because you believe you don't deserve anything at all. Ask for more, ask for much more, never settle for anything.

Only those who love themselves can be persistent; self-love is reflected in their consistent actions. Persistent focus on a goal, while continuing to move forward, will sooner or later lead to success.

START READING HERE

The best way to kill your dreams is to give up as soon as you stumble. Break with the habit of giving up. Stop putting useless material into your mind, heart, habits, and home. Do away with junk thoughts. Thoughts are powerful when combined with a clear purpose, perseverance, faith, and discipline.

Our minds constantly focus on the five most prevalent thoughts, directing our focus toward that vision. What thoughts do you have? How do you approach them? And what motivates you to think in that way?

Do not answer yet. Think, analyze, meditate, and repeat. You are what you think. Spend 10 minutes a day thinking and meditating on what kind of person you want to become. Do it with true focus and commitment. Introduce perseverance and repetition into your life, make good thoughts a consistent part of your day, and you will start to experience all aspects of life to the fullest. Every negative thought becomes a contaminated emotion, and a contaminated emotion will engender harmful acts and habits.

What a great moment in life when you stop pretending and start being!

When you think, sow it; when you feel, water it; when you act, reap it. Instead of getting exhausted from losing faith, get exhausted from overcoming challenges.

Repetition is at the core of character and skill. Practice and perfect your art. Generate new habits and train your discipline. Consistency enables you to identify the error and correct it. Repetition serves to highlight and overcome obstacles, enabling you to replace a "no" with a "yes"; it involves a series of "setbacks" that ultimately result in success. Fail, but don't fail to Olympic levels, no one celebrates their mistakes, just what they learn from them; you must be able to grab them by the scruff of the neck and let them know that you will never let them happen again. Get rid of them, and make room for others.

Self-love does not mean pride, and perseverance does not suggest that you should keep going without taking time to appreciate the present and reflect on your mistakes. One reason why many stumbling blocks hinder our transformation is because we so eagerly want to move on to the next chapter that we don't pause to consider seriously what we have experienced.

We are in such a hurry to get out of the situation and move on to what's next, that we don't reflect on what we have experienced. We do everything in a hurry, everything is urgent, but nothing is so important that we cannot stop to analyze what we spent our time doing and, above all, who did we do it for? Consider how you spend your time, and whether every moment of your life is stitched into eternity and not into something fleeting, such as your earthly existence, then you are on the right track.

We want quick results, and consistency is at odds with impatience. The world provides us with countless conveniences, and our minds are increasingly devoted to being subservient to them. We have developed a sense of entitlement, convincing ourselves that even minimal effort should result in us reaping the rewards of life. How much progress have we truly made in fulfilling this expectation? Is our success genuine? Human progress has not been achieved by adhering to established molds and structures, but rather by challenging them and pursuing new opportunities with a relentless drive to avoid mediocrity. Being consistent is a virtue that few apply and is fundamental for everything.

Repetition without learning is the purest of follies.

The exercise I want to leave you with for this chapter will last several days, and it cannot be otherwise if we want to develop perseverance, but it is not complicated, if we could just understand that what is complex is almost never complicated. It goes like this: in the box on page 132, you are going to write every day, for two weeks, everything you have done toward your dreams. Do it before bedtime or early the next day, if it makes it easier, but avoid putting it off beyond that.

On those days when you do not do something specific, indicate why. What stopped you? What was it that was more important than your dreams?

I invite you to adopt this exercise beyond the time established here. Do it daily and come back to it every week or month. See how much you have done to live in body and soul, and how much you have done to just feed the body.

Sometimes all it takes is a little effort to break out of the slumber that keeps you from your full potential. The unbreakable are always willing to risk everything, they don't look for guarantees, they would rather embrace failure than think they might miss out on an opportunity in life. Keep moving forward, even if that means enduring great injury along the way.

Always move forward, because the back is already full.

They will say it was luck, but it's consistency. They'll chalk it up to chance, but it's discipline. They will think it was a fad, but it's actually a trend resulting from your tireless work. They will call it intelligence, but it's wisdom. They will think it was a miracle, but it's grace.

Stop asking vague and confused questions, the Lord will respond to that which is clear and specific. It will not be enough just to have faith at the beginning, you must maintain it until you see your prayers being answered.

You will be like a rock: though beaten and covered by the turbulent waters, you will emerge from the white foam triumphant, the waves come and go, but you will always remain. Trust even without strength, feed on the eternal and you will fly, no matter what.

Don't stop fighting. Don't think that the things I have achieved, whether many or few, were achieved by themselves. Very few achieve goals without effort, and usually these goals do not last very long. I have chosen a continuous path. Those who think that one day I decided to become a lecturer and writer, and everything else came as if by magic, are mistaken.

Being unbreakable is not established by decree. It is a constant challenge, I did a lot before writing these pages with you, I do it while you write your part, and I will do it in the future because otherwise I would no longer be who I am.

I am not yet 40 years old, and I have racked up a career spanning almost 30 years, including almost 20 years as an entrepreneur and businessman. I am here thanks to my successes and, above all, my failures. I have dedicated myself to the

It's funny how they call me a dreamer when I sleep so little.

131

	What did you do for your dreams?	**Nothing?** What stopped you? What was so important?
Day 1		
Day 2		
Day 3		
Day 4		
Day 5		
Day 6		
Day 7		

	What did you do for your dreams?	**Nothing?** What stopped you? What was so important?
Day 8		
Day 9		
Day 10		
Day 11		
Day 12		
Day 13		
Day 14		

professional, business, and human domains. I have used pain as one of my construction tools.

I took that pain and turned it into consistency. I share this with deep love and genuine humility. I write it here with the intention of showing that it can be done, but not overnight. At that time, I continually thought that it would never happen, yet I persisted unwaveringly, even when faced with the imminent danger of the precipice of the waterfall.

When I talk about my challenges, whether they be struggles or failures, it is not to highlight suffering or affliction; rather it is to stress that the time and effort invested in pursuing your goals will ultimately be the most fulfilling in your life. If this is not the case, maybe you are not on the right path. If you are doing what you really love, you will not need a vacation, those who pursue their passions do not distinguish between Monday and Friday. Who wants to take a break when you are doing what fills your soul?

Opportunities didn't just fall into my lap; I had to put in the effort and work tirelessly to create them. While others were making grand promises and socializing every week from Thursday to Sunday, I was working tirelessly from Monday to Sunday, pursuing my dreams.

I'm not going to repeat the story that I sold everything from lollipops to sandwiches, you already know about that. It's important to remember that I was wrong hundreds of times, that on multiple occasions I was the worst employee, the worst boss, and even the worst son. The consequences of my passion and temperament were not always positive; my rigorous way of dealing with fear led me to great successes, but also to some resounding failures.

I treasure the memory of the humiliations and the doors slammed in my face. I rose through the ranks to become the director of nine

companies and the leader of hundreds of employees. From that height I plummeted to the bottom of the abyss. And there was God, who is everywhere, shaping me deeply in the wilderness. I am infinitely grateful to have made it there.

I will continue to struggle, because this story does not end until God types the final period point. In the meantime, I will continue to branch out beyond my apparent talents and gifts, I want to go places where others do not go because the price is too high; but I assure you that I have received more blessings for being disciplined and determined than for all my talents combined.

It doesn't matter how hard you try, what matters is how many times you come back and do it again.

Those who accompany me are guided and supported by His right hand. It is important for you to know that He will do the same for you, because He loves us all equally. Don't fail Him, love yourself and win that battle.

DON'T TOLERATE

The thousands and thousands of geniuses who go unrecognized and live in bankruptcy. People who did not even reach a fifth of what they could have been. Your talents and gifts are a vehicle, they are a path, they are powerful construction tools, but they are of no use if they are not accompanied by constancy, the ability to execute, a fierce will, and clarity of purpose. It is these factors, above and beyond your talents, that will ensure your resilience in the face of the adversities that you are certain to face.

Stop tolerating that which neither blesses you nor adds to you. Being tolerant is often a problem:

Tolerating mediocrity will sooner or later make you mediocre.

Tolerating evil will sooner or later lead you to accept evil.

Tolerating fear will sooner or later turn you into a fearful person.

Tolerating your poverty is to accept it and live it as if it were by design.

Countless young and ambitious individuals consign themselves to destitution and misfortune by heeding the remarks of those who have destined them for a life of misery.

If only you knew that you are the sole cause of your own misfortune, that the redundancy of tainted ideas has denied you prosperity. They are the parasites of your subconscious, they feed on your will and from there they determine the quality of your thoughts and emotions, they take them to the physical plane where, through you, they give shape to that negative reality that once only existed in your mind.

Get the hell up! Stop crying, your time is running out. Every day of limitations you tolerate is one day less to fulfill your dreams. And while you're complaining, someone else is eating your lunch. Raise the standards of your life, stop indulging your mistakes, expel apathy and bad habits, stop accepting abuse, stop allowing someone else to steal what belongs to you. Stop being tolerant. Stop saying: "This is the way I had to live", "these are my circumstances", "my grandfather was a loser" or "my dad is a loser, and I will be a loser too".

Don't tolerate. If you were born poor it will be a challenge, but if you die poor, it will be your responsibility, because your spirit is a treasure.

Live more, exert yourself more, and give more, there is no such thing as overnight success, so be aggressive and go after what you want!

Stop tolerating, and don't ever give up again.

Chapter 9

Human torches

I believe in my heart, which is always poured out, but never emptied.

Gabriela Mistral

So far we have been talking about us, packing your backpack with the basics you need for the road ahead. Now it's time to focus on you, but this time we are going to introduce some items that will allow you to be closer to those you want to support.

In some circles, the role of the motivational speaker is held in disdain as if it were just a simple task, one that consists simply of combining powerful phrases that bring a tear to the eye or raise a smile, with no real impact on the spirits of those who hear them. Many would argue that it sounds simple, but there are moments when challenging circumstances can overwhelm our motivation to move forward.

I wonder why you need motivation. Isn't living enough?

And you will say:

"Listen, Daniel, if you knew what my life has been like, you wouldn't call it living."

And I would agree with you:

"It's true, there are some people who, despite having been dead for 20 years, are still walking around."

What happened to you? What did you lose, your job? Well, go and get yourself another one. A love, then go out and fall in love with yourself this time.

Did they abandon you? did they betray you? did you make a mistake? You can choose whether to hold on to these things, or you can embrace the idea that fresh possibilities have been made available to you.

If you don't have any money, then it's time to be creative, to innovate. You now have an enormous advantage over those who have already made their fortune, because they are more likely to be afraid of losing it. You will not face the same hardships that others have endured, trapped in a cycle of previous successes. You are free to choose the adventure and leave the mundane to them. What is life if not an incredible journey filled with challenges, difficulties, and, of course, some moments of peace? Leaders

Not all those who are buried lived.

IF LIFE IS TRYING TO

KILL YOU,

LET IT SHOOT.

are forged through challenges and adversity, no one wants to create something only to leave it sitting idle.

It's time for a change. If you've been the same all your life, don't you think it's time to be better? I don't want you to do it when you finish reading this page, or in a month. I want you to do it now: put the book down and do it now, make something new happen.

He who is willing to stake his life on his convictions is destined for success.

You're full of gifts and talents, but you don't know where to find them. Stop putting yourself down because of the way your body or nose looks, or because of the size of your stomach or your thinning hair. Stop complaining about being poor, not having a degree or because you feel the years are catching up with you. If you told your friends the things you tell yourself, would you have many friends left? If you could eat your words would they be nourishing or poisonous?

I know it's challenging and requires effort, but if someone put a gun to your head and forced you to change, wouldn't you do everything possible to make that change? Isn't that the way life works? It compels you to respond, because it's only through adversity that we learn to overcome challenges. It is during times like these that you have to take the required action, so that each step moves you closer to your goal. Instead of relying on a wish list, focus on mastering your own thoughts and using them to serve your spiritual growth.

Love your scars, show off your scratches and fractures, use them to your advantage. You cannot conquer new lands with the soul of a victim. Go and fight your battle! You decide who you are, not your circumstances, not other people. What's in the past, is in the past. Nothing is permanent. Don't view your current circumstances as the ultimate outcome.

If you want greatness, stop asking for permission and go for it without giving a damn what anyone thinks of you. They will try to dictate your future, but the power behind your future lies with you. Stay hungry, crush pain, eradicate bitterness, and quell anger. Remove the bitterness from your being. To be able to forgive, you must first learn to forgive yourself. Do not fall into folly, because every battle is a personal struggle that you must fight alone.

Don't live the life you have, live the life you want.

Understanding what motivates you is crucial, especially if you are trying to help others. You need to understand clearly that when you provide support to someone, you are helping them achieve their goals, not dragging them down into ditches dug by others.

It is a terrible thing to strive to meet everyone's expectations and then allowing those expectations to have mastery over us. We feel obliged to comply with the whims of our parents, teachers, partners, and social circles. Even nowadays I know people (some even older than me) who struggle with the decision of either conforming to their parents' wishes or pursuing their own ambitions instead. Others oscillate between doubt, low self-esteem, and fear of *what people will say* and are eager to indulge the thoughts and whims of others.

Those who live this way sometimes succeed in satisfying others, but never in satisfying themselves.

Allowing yourself to be influenced by opinions will only lead you away from your purpose. These days, there are millions of entrepreneurs of all ages who have consigned themselves to poverty or misfortune because of some offhand criticism or remarks that were allowed to become a preordained sentence of complete failure. Those who could once have been entrepreneurs, now burned at the stake of discredit and mistrust, are convinced that there is an alien force that they cannot control, leaving them with the feeling that they are inevitable heirs to ruin.

Neither sickness, nor poverty, nor loneliness, nor death: rather to live without purpose is the greatest of tragedies.

For thousands of years, the greatest philosophers have argued about the meaning of life. Philosophy is an invaluable field of study, but when it comes to concepts regarding our existence, we don't venture beyond the speculative. You will not find your purpose behind every door marked "Success". We are who we choose to be, and the circumstances of the world are shaped by our own decisions. You may have lost everything, but you can still build it all back over time.

I like to think that we all have the potential to be like the flame of a torch in the darkness, shining brightly, never going out, despite the headwinds. One whose radiance comes from its purpose, which is simply to light another torch, with the ultimate goal being to kindle a flame that guides the path for all of us. What ignites a flame within you is what you will radiate outward.

All lights illuminate, but not all provide warmth. There are those who walk blindly because they walk by the light of others, lacking their own inner light. This is why many have emerged from the darkness, but the darkness still remains in them. They will tell you that you are not capable, that you are a loser, an exile, you are persecuted, impure, condemned, a sinner, a failure, a fool, or weak. But you do not belong to the darkness.

It is when you behave authentically, without any masks or pretense, that change starts to happen. Stop focusing on what has no meaning or value, avoid maximizing your shortcomings, stop crying and using these things as an excuse. Pay no attention to what others think of you; you must learn to know yourself, but never turn your back on advice or wisdom, you must learn to listen without it becoming a distraction.

Look in the mirror, and if you see a coward tell him where to go, because there is no room in your heart for both of you.

Make the effort! Be brave! You won't get there any other way. Be fearless, this life will eat cowards for breakfast. Put all your trust in your faith and learn to see yourself as God sees you.

I want to pass on to you the formula that has guided my life during all these years of falling down and getting back up, of falling apart and healing, of sinking down to the bottom and rising back up again. Throughout all that time I have been guided by one unfailing ratio:

145

51% imagination + 49% hard work.

Bearing that combination in mind, take some time to answer these questions:

What could you do 24 hours a day without getting paid?

What would you do if you had what, according to you, you don't have today?

What's the worst that could happen if you try?

What determines your actions?

Now I want you to think seriously about your answers. You don't have to write it down, but you can if you want to.

Is there anything that you would do for pure pleasure?

It's okay to write "no" for an answer. Not everyone knows what they want, not everyone has their purpose clearly defined. Don't be embarrassed, but you do need to have a long session alone with yourself. If you still don't know what it is, there is a direction that, if you follow it, will help you find out: By serving others, you will discover a never-ending source of peace, joy, and happiness, gaining gratitude and wisdom along the way.

Save your answer, and we'll come back and look at it soon.

Is there really anything that you need in order to accomplish what you want to do?

If someone gave you the money today that you need to start the business that you are so enthusiastic about, would you start it or would you just keep the money? Sometimes it's not so much the project that we want as the pleasures it would bring us. It's great to have money, but it's much better when we earn it by doing something that also fulfills our souls. If I were to put all the money you need for your project in one hand and all the pleasure you would get from it in the other, which one would you choose?

Would the result of taking action lead to a very different life than the one you have today?

It is important to remember we often don't do what we want to do because we are afraid of consequences, but the consequences are no worse than the life we have now. That's the mindset that leaves us tied to miserable jobs for years, traps us in abusive relationships that only bring us unhappiness, and convinces us to accept a life devoid of excitement when we could be overflowing with happiness and laughter.

When faced with the question of what dictates your life, just think to yourself: Is it really something that's worth the sacrifice? If you have put God in that category, then yes, it's worth it. Are you sure you would behave the same way if it were God guiding your actions?

If your answer is yes, there's no need to answer the next question:

Are you happy?

☐ Yes

☐ No

If the tunnel is dark,
be the light that

ILLUMINATES IT.

SURROUND YOURSELF WITH GIANTS

Surround yourself with spiritual giants and not with mental dwarfs. The gossipers and critics will always come across as more attractive and, possibly, more interesting, because they live in a state of mindless rebellion.

The world says: "Divide and conquer", but the positive formula is: "Unite and multiply". Understand: the individual will always be crushed by a crowd that goes against them. Some people are so good at making excuses that they will never be good at success; those feckless people who cannot accept the consequences of their actions, and for whom everything that happens is always out of their hands, blame others and fabricate arguments to justify their own ruin.

If you decide to party every night and sleep in every morning, watch TV during the day, spend your time waiting for the weekend, and wind up complaining about everything, without giving it your all, I only have one thing to say: don't feel sorry for yourself when that routine comes knocking at your door and takes root in your life. We cannot regret the decisions we make when we know what we're doing.

If you don't know the difference between "frequent" and "infrequent" it's because you *frequently* watch television and *infrequently* open a book. It's time to change, to live a life of growth. Who wants to be like they were yesterday?

If you are one of those who say: "Well, if she's going to love me, let her love me as I am." Well, no! If you are a rude, obnoxious lout; if you are a liar; if you don't shower every day; if you don't use deodorant and can't be bothered with personal grooming; if you don't work and go out in dirty clothes; if you are an arrogant, overbearing imbecile; if you promise to do anything for her, but you don't even do the basics; if you don't show any interest in progress and you accumulate vices as if you were collecting them; if you're not thorough, don't have a plan, and don't feel passion, don't expect anyone to love you "just the way you are".

Rise up! You are a giant, but first you have to do away with the dwarf who controls you.

They can break my legs, arms, or ribs, but they can never break my spirit, and when I say "never", I mean "NEVER". Time stands still and completely loses its value.

Many years ago, when I was going through one of the worst crises of my life, I remember seeing my reflection in a broken mirror, and I realized that the hardships I'd been through had drastically changed me from how I used to be. I remembered that we are all built to soar, but sometimes, for fear of being called "crazy", we hesitate and listen to those who crawl. That reflection told me how brief life is.

I learned that to be a giant I must first kneel down before the Lord and give my life to the giant of the cosmos. He gathered the broken and the worn, buffed them against the hardest stone, and appointed me as leader during the turmoil. Then he healed my wounds, brushed my wings, and sent me out to slay titans.

I am always filled with intense passion, it's more than just a feeling or a show; it is a powerful burst of energy within me, a passion that comes from the mysterious chemistry within my soul, that causes an uncontrollable reaction that overpowers my rationality; it's not driven by emotions but by the strength of the human spirit.

Every day more and more of us hear the sound of the trumpet and shout: "Here we are, ready for battle, victorious in a world that has already lost!"

Surround yourself with spiritual giants.

When you think of your dreams and doubt begins to sap your vision, crush that uncertainty with the promises of the Eternal.

Remain steadfast, hold on to life and faith. Tomorrow the sun will rise in all its glory, it may rise behind the clouds, but one thing is for sure, it will rise.

I have fought with the Judases, but in the end, they bring about their own downfall.

Your emotional weakness can be overcome through spiritual strength: when you find God, the search ends, but the journey begins.

Chapter 10

Climb like a sherpa

Men wanted for hazardous journey. Low wages.
Bitter cold. Long hours of complete darkness.
Constant danger. Safe return doubtful. Honor
and recognition in the event of success.

Ernest Shackleton

I n the previous chapter we wrote about the things that bring fullness to our souls, and how from them we must get the traction we need to move forward through the swamps and deserts that we have to cross. We will now review the factors that allow us to bridge the gap between our motivation and how we can motivate others.

The only name I know to describe those who bring out the best in their environment is "leaders". Leadership is not a trait or a rank, it is not a position or an occupation. Leadership is a decision, a sacrifice, and a vocation. It is a package that is worth taking a chance on.

Leadership comes at a price: give your all for others.

Don't think that this chapter is not for you because you don't have a team to lead in the formal sense, or if you are still on the bottom of your company's hierarchy. Leadership transcends these positions so that you decide how big a space you want to inspire. I have taught courses and workshops in hundreds of companies, and on countless occasions I find leaders with no position or title beyond the extent of their passion and greatness of the example they set.

In business, we devote a certain amount of time to leadership, the same principles also apply when it comes to your family, your school group, your community, or any other social group to which you belong.

I would like you to erase from your mind the image of the leader as a person sitting in an office. Most of them are bosses, not leaders, much less mentors. Don't equate a politician or a religious leader with your definition of leadership just because thousands of people follow them. That is fame or popularity. Leadership should not be measured by the number of followers, but by the positive transformations that you are able to generate in them, by the advances that each individual makes for himself and by what he is able to inspire in the collective.

If your
dreams
are

TOO BIG,

don't
disclose
them to
small minds.

Just because you have authority over someone does not mean you are their leader. The gap between leadership and authority is huge, because if you are not willing to stand up for those who follow you, then you do not deserve that they walk shoulder to shoulder with you, no matter how big the sign on the wall establishing their authority.

Love is a process that comes from synergy: the more it is shared, the more it is reinforced and multiplied. Nowhere is too far away when it comes to serving. Someone who is unbreakable will never be too tired or think it is too late when there is a chance to go forward and love someone. Treating people fairly and demonstrating humanity are two characteristics that should define them. With these principles, they will establish an iron discipline, applied with righteousness and excellence.

Although leadership rooted in love is understood as surrender, it is not an easy journey. Whoever dreams of becoming a leader must get used to the laughter and criticism. There will always be people willing to stop others from daring to do what they would never even attempt.

Never allow the opinions of others to deter you, remain steadfast in your direction and persevere in the face of obstacles. Remember that a broken dream can also serve as the building block for an even bigger one. Muttering has no place in a mind strengthened by clear objectives, there will always be someone who seeks to undermine you, who criticizes you because they don't have your talents or your gifts, people who fantasize about being able to conquer without effort what you conquered through hard work. Unable to surpass you, they will try to bring you down to their level. They are like crabs, and they will continue to be weak if they do not change their mindset and beliefs.

When I decided to break out of the mold, I knew what to expect. I knew I would face slings and arrows, but ultimately, the driving force behind the love and support that propels me forward comes from the guidance that I receive from the Master. That is all I need to stand strong, because smart minds, and spirits imbued from on high, are always ready to learn, they always have their ears

Those who seek knowledge just want to be like *books*. Those who embrace wisdom want to be *free*.

open to understanding, and never stray from their life's purpose.

The first step to leading others is to lead yourself. Following someone who doesn't know their own direction is fruitless. A leader who does not have a defined destiny, nor a mapped-out route, will end up being diluted among the crowd.

In the specific case of leadership in companies and organizations, a leader must stand up for people, without making excuses: the leader takes responsibility for the mistakes and errors of those he is working to train.

This aspect is of vital importance because, in spite of being a loving and firm leader of character, the error is not always in the leader, who must strive forward with unwavering confidence. This reminds me of Judas, who learned from the best teacher, the ultimate leader. Although he shared the passion and vision with others, he failed to change his ways and chose an easier path without challenges, despite knowing he was the source of his own downfall.

I'll give you an example: you choose friends and family for a business venture because you trust them and that's all you can afford, but it turns out they don't have the skills to do the work you assign them. So, you look for people who are qualified to run your business, but you don't trust them and they don't share your passion. Thus, finding people who have the skills, who are trustworthy, and who, at the same time, share your passion to operate and grow your company, will not only be your job, but also a responsibility inherent in your leadership. Furthermore, a key element will be the motivation you can infuse into the lifeblood of your team. If you are the leader and you complain about them, the person that needs to change is you.

Building on from the earlier example, tough and difficult decisions will need to be made in order to progress in your career; not all of your friends and family may be suitable to join your team, because the bigger the picture, the higher the standards must be of those who want to be part of that picture. You need to choose people who add value and meaning, and who don't just do their job.

Therefore, be prepared for the trials and tribulations, the slings and the arrows that will come with trusting and giving the benefit of the doubt to friends and family members. Without neglecting your feelings, you need to create a family that functions like a high-performing team by combining love and discipline together.

Once you reach the next level, it's important to recognize that complacency can be a major obstacle when it comes to motivating a team. People who fear stepping out of their comfort zone are likely to resist progress, disrupt productivity, and create challenges for both you as the leader and their team. These will be the ones who spread stories of failure and cause panic in the face of uncertainty, they must be uprooted immediately, before they grow like thorns that suffocate everyone else's vision.

Peace will be the arbiter of your decisions.

A true leader improves on yesterday's mistakes on a daily basis, doesn't accept not having made progress in every interaction, and makes demands on himself before making demands on others. Lead by example with your actions, don't allow the mediocrity of others to diminish your desire for excellence.

Assertiveness is fundamental, together with the deep intuition of your spirit, in tune with your heart and mind; they are your navigational guide to making decisions as a leader. Not everyone will make it to the top, particularly if they have already been warned and persist in repeating their errors, leading to levels of risk that are unsustainable. You will have to be as cool as the situation demands, and weigh the consequences of keeping them on the team, and when you feel bad about having to make a decision to let go of those who get in the way and conspire against the collective project, remember that while that one person may have to leave, they can always be replaced by someone who is motivated to succeed.

When you're down, those who stay put will be there wanting to see you fall, but the difference is that you had a real adventure while theirs was a wish that didn't go beyond "It could have been".

And in the end you will descend, like a sherpa, like a guide who leads others to the top of Everest and then descends in wholesome peace, not missing what he has left at the top, for the pleasure of leading others is like no other.

Don't become a leader who accumulates followers, be the one who builds up leaders. It is time to sow, water, and harvest leaders. Conformity is a disease in the business world, but also in our educational system, in our interaction with institutions and politics.

If we do not change the people around us, if we do not prepare them to become masters of their own destiny, they will end up devoured by the wolves, and we will end up alongside them. This is a role that you must combine along with your passion, it is a burden that you must delight in taking on. If you're not willing to risk anything for others, or change yourself so that they progress, you don't deserve to lead anyone. The common trait of the greatest social transformers is that they have devoted their lives to the betterment of many others. There are many examples, but what about Jesus? He is the only leader I know who was the exact embodiment of His message.

If you don't know how to smile, laugh, love, forgive, help, serve, teach, you are not a leader, you are just a boss. Leadership is a two-way exchange, you have to learn to receive in order to grow with what you share.

This time, I don't want to take you through a long and complex exercise. On the contrary, this one will be very simple.

I want you to answer two short questionnaires and plot the results on a graph.

No one is emptier than a person who is full of himself.

I will answer a sample question, and you can reply to the rest.

On a scale of 1 to 5, where 1 is *Not at all important* and 5 is *Very important*, how important is it for you that a leader has:

	1	2	3	4	5
Focus on results					

Imagine you consider that being *focused on results* is important for a leader, but not to an extreme extent, you can give it a four (4).

	1	2	3	4	5
Focus on results				✓	

Then, you will look for "Focus on Results" in the chart at the end of the chapter and put a dot on the four.

We will look for the 4 in the criterion we are evaluating and mark it.

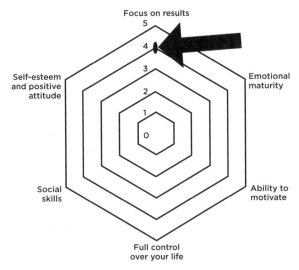

When you have finished answering all the questions, you will connect the dots and get an image like this one:

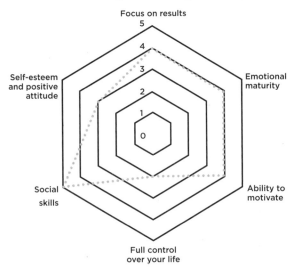

When you do this, you will answer another simple questionnaire; you will repeat the process and draw the second line, with a different color; it will look like this:

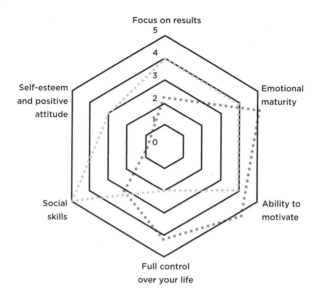

The idea is that at the end you compare both evaluations; you will compare the leadership attributes and lines.

Now that you know what to do, you can answer the questions:

On a scale of 1 to 5, where 1 is *Not at all important* and 5 is *Very important*, how important is it for you that a leader has:

	1	2	3	4	5
Emotional maturity					
Ability to motivate					
Focus on results					
Social skills					
Self-esteem and positive attitude					
Full control over their life					

Once you have put the dots on the graph at the end of the chapter and joined them together to make the first line, go back and complete the following questions:

On a scale of 1 to 5, where 1 is *Not at all important* and 5 is *Very important*, how do you think the people around you would evaluate you on each of these attributes?

	1	2	3	4	5
Emotional maturity					
Ability to motivate					
Focus on results					
Social skills					
Self-esteem and positive attitude					
Full control over their life					

I think you've already guessed it. When you line up this second set of questions, you will have a comparison between your ideal leader and where you are. Well, there will be a number of differences that you should look at.

For example, imagine that you considered self-esteem as very important and gave it a 5, but in the self-assessment let's say you gave yourself a 3. So in this example, *self-esteem* would be an area that you have to look at.

I repeat, leadership is important in all facets of your life, not only in your professional or business life. Review your attributes and start leading the climb to the top.

If you want to take this exercise further, you can add new criteria to your list of attributes. Remember that if you include too many attributes you make the interpretation of the graph more complicated, but if you include too few, you will only have

I prefer people who are
more willing than those
who just have

EXCUSES:

a limited overview of your capabilities. If you want to try it, here is a list of options that you can work with:

Spiritual development

Academic training

Creativity

Boldness

Prudence

Ability to dream

Being realistic

Healthy sense of humor

Consistency in the balance between
    private and public life

Personal appearance

CLIMB LIKE A SHERPA

The purpose of our lives is often hidden from us. During those moments, we walk cautiously with fear, as if navigating through the thick darkness of a foggy early morning. When this happens, our decision-making wavers and we become blinded by anguish, we are unable to make the most important decisions with any certainty or wisdom.

Do not despair, whenever anxiety overwhelms you in the midst of apparent abandonment, the more assurance you should have that the Master is in control of every step of the way. Regardless of how big your problem, anguish, or fear. He has mastery over the situation, even if you can't see it.

Let me ask you something. What is holding you back? For how long have you longed to see the summit and said to yourself: "I wish I could be there"? You can either look at the peaks of your life today as obstacles or as opportunities; the choice is yours. You can either give in to your fears or continue on the climb. That decision is also yours.

Resilience will enable you to adjust to the radical and unfair changes that life throws at you. Your strength and spiritual depth are demonstrated through your ability to keep getting back on your feet, validated by the desire to go on, even if you don't see the peak, even if the goal remains hidden behind the dense fog.

Even if you are thousands of miles away, it is not the distance that separates you from the top, but fear, laziness, apathy, and despondency that determine the size of the gap. Don't give up, even if it all seems in vain. Carry on.

And when you put your boots on and decide to start up the slope again, climb like a sherpa, and take others with you.

Climb like a sherpa, don't go alone.

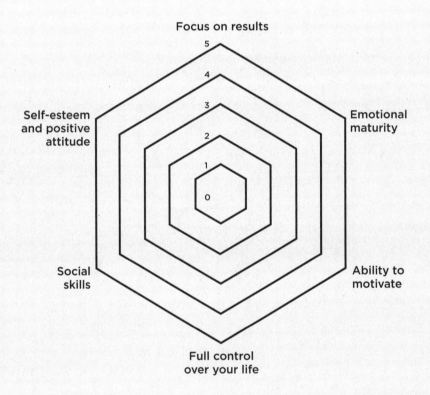

Chapter 11

To define yourself is to limit yourself

And once the storm is over, you won't remember how you made it, how you survived. You won't even be sure if the storm is really over. One thing is for sure, though: when you come out of that storm, you won't be the same person who walked into it.

Haruki Murakami

The first step in being able to influence those around you is to bring about a change in yourself. In the last chapter, we discussed how some people expect others to make huge progress, yet they themselves are reluctant to even take one simple step. Setting an example is the most powerful weapon to help others; in order to become agents of change, it is essential to first undertake a personal transformation in all areas of one's own life.

This change is that fight we were talking about a few pages ago, it is that battle in which a better version of you tears you down, imposes itself, and emerges victorious.

Most of us go through life focusing on limitations, we dance to the beat of others. The unbreakable think and live to overcome themselves.

You worry about temporary problems when you have an ever-lasting God.

We believe that change implies losing something, but losing what feeds our defiled habits and destroys us, even when it gives us pleasure, is an excellent way of winning.

Human beings often make the mistake of relying on danger to justify their existence or simply just to feel alive. That is why we reward ourselves with the things that hurt us. We don't weigh the consequences because they are not usually in the present, they are in the future, and we believe that we will deal with them down the line, but the reality is quite different. Our life is driven by reactions to pain and pleasure, instead of being driven by wisdom, spirit, or a deep understanding of the mind.

We should not allow everything that takes place around us to determine the circumstances, quality, and trajectory of our life. We react to external conflicts in the same way as we deal with internal ones. By focusing inward instead of outward, you

THEY ARE SO NEEDY

that they see small stones
as a stumbling block.

will see that you are more willing to do something to avoid pain than to feel pleasure.

How many times have you said "no" knowing that you should answer "yes", just because you thought your pride was at stake? Wrongly associated emotions create misguided habits that the intellect cannot break no matter how hard the mind tries.

There is nothing more foolish than saying: "This is just how I am." What if "being that way" is the reason you're not able to become who you want to be? How many times have your soul, your heart, and your spirit agreed that you need a change and then your mind takes over and says: "That's just the way I am, and I'm not going to change"? That is the exact definition of foolishness. This is a violent perversion, which brings misery to our life. We are not aware of the profound and terrible impact it has. Foolishness can lead us to lose everything. It is much more than a behavioral trait, it is the result of living, growing up, and acting like fools. Foolishness is sustained by your pride, and pride is sustained by low self-esteem.

Foolishness can be debilitating when it is fueled by both ignorance and pride.

Perhaps you find it painful to accept this perspective, but when these desires to be disobedient arise, you feel that your attitude is not within the bounds of your control, and you realize that you have unwittingly adopted a position of a certain hypocrisy that seeks to justify something that you are not, while keeping your spirit imprisoned in the mask that you have insisted on wearing, however uncomfortable it feels.

The most convincing proof that someone is wearing a suit that is not tailored for them is that their heart is showing at the seams. This is most evident when you find yourself arguing with a fool and the first thing he does is to justify himself, then he calls you weak and tries to cause you harm.

You can have a discussion with all kinds of people and draw something nourishing from the conversation, except with those who are foolish. Your arguments will be futile, they will only use them as ammunition to attack you back. There are those who deserve an explanation, there are those who deserve an answer, and there are those who only deserve your silence.

If you are living a life of foolishness, change. If you are one of those who remained stagnant and said: "This is just the way I am, this is the way I have always been, and this is the way I will die", you should know that every time you say those words you sign your own death certificate: it means that you have given up the privilege of growing and have forgotten that you are here to generate value.

"Danny, I want a divorce. My marriage is no longer working," a senior executive at one of the companies I advise told me.

"I'm sorry to hear that," I replied. "And why do you feel that your relationship is no longer working?"

"She has changed so much."

"And what about you?"

"I haven't changed, not me. I'm still the same."

"Well, that's the problem," I said directly, without softening the blow.

Who wants to stay the same in a world that changes so quickly?

Everything has changed: technology, airplanes, phones, satellites, cars, fashion. And when are you going to change? Why stay the same?

Nothing is forever: not tragedies, not mistakes, not fears, and not pain. You should know that your current situation is not forever either, and that is something you should be thankful for. The more you resist, the more it will hurt to change when it becomes an unavoidable reality.

Refusing to suffer generates much more damage than the change itself. Your transformation might cause you some discomfort, but it will only be temporary, whereas the discomfort you inflict on yourself as a consequence of your resistance will last for as long as you refuse to make the change. There is nothing more dangerous than feeling safe. Show bravery and tenacity in the face of difficulties and shortcomings. You can turn fear into power, tear up the scripted answers, and erase the entire script that you had written for yourself. Never deny the small changes in your life.

You either change or pay the consequences of staying the same.

Stop longing for what you had and use what you have. Grow up, do your hair however you want, tighten your belt, sharpen your mind, and blow the trumpets that mark the beginning of a new battle. You will recover double what you lost.

In order to change, you have to know how to choose the right words. These words carry with them light and power, as long as they are used wisely. Some words are uplifting while others are destructive. They can also determine fate for those who are selective with the right vocabulary. There are expressions and voices of power, success, and blessing. With the right words we make people laugh or cry, we hurt or heal, by using the right language we can sell and negotiate, but words are also there to bring about great transformations in us.

How we speak to the face in the mirror each morning will define how the rest of the day will go. Likewise, the way we speak to our spirit will determine what we will experience on each journey. Words have been used to transform the path of history and the destiny of nations.

Words represent our emotions, but above all they are actions that begin the river of our thoughts, whose course, if not controlled and mastered, ends up drowning us in the wrong emotions. This is why we should be careful with our words, and closely examine what comes out of our mouths. Miracles are contained within your words. Stop cursing the darkness and instead bless the light to come forth. Change your world by changing your words.

Find the best terms to express yourself and communicate with others, try to expand your vocabulary through reading, and say what you have always said, but in a different way. Store words up with power and use them to impart power to others: linguistics shapes our mind and emotions, it is a way of expressing the same but with better results.

I love thinking about the great authors: Alighieri, Shakespeare, Octavio Paz, García Márquez, Ovid, Bolaño, Neruda, Nicanor Parra, Angelou, Mistral (excerpts from several of them are found throughout this book), or all those that you like and that give you goose bumps. With their writings, these greats succeeded in describing existence and beauty in a way that gives them an even greater quality: the definition of a tree in the voice of these poets would seem like an everlasting description. Imagine then the definition of something as formidable as your life.

What goes into our mouth can defile our body; what comes out of our mouth defiles our soul.

It brings power and majesty to your life; a single word can give you the feeling of revival in your own being.

Listen and you will feel the enormous difference between saying "I do things well" and saying "I do things impeccably", the difference between "striving for the best" and "achieving excellence". When you think of something that you find "disgusting" and relabel it with another term, such as "peculiar" or "extraordinary", your mind becomes divided and confused between labels and emotions.

You can break through the labels by transforming the words, if you have a limited and poor vocabulary, it's quite likely that your wallet will be the same. This may be a harsh and uncomfortable truth. But you must face it.

Whenever a person speaks, everyone in the room knows exactly what books he reads, if any, and of what nature his interests and delights are. The easiest way to access your emotions is through the labels we place on our feelings and experiences; if you only have a few labels, the nuances with which you will appreciate your surroundings will also be scarce.

This doesn't make educated or well-read people better, but it does mean that they will have greater resources to interpret the world around them. We will return to this subject later, because there are people who are well educated, but who have very little wisdom.

The labels that you can attach are the flavors, music, smells, and textures of life put into words; with these labels you can bridge the gap between emotion and cognition. There is always something that you would like to change, or an attitude that we can't change from one day to the next. In this chapter we will change the exercise to an experiment, I do want you to do this, but I won't be responsible if you end up writing the rest of the book from the asylum. I'll tell you how it works:

Letting go of the stagnation of negative thoughts is the simplest and most natural action for the brain to take.

We cannot label ourselves with adjectives that don't derive from constant habit. This means, you can't claim to be kind unless you are kind as a matter of practice. There's no such thing as an instantaneous habit, they all require a process of adaptation, some taking more time than others, but it will never be immediate.

The experiment involves forcing yourself to become the thing you want to be. For example, suppose you are a person with a bad temper. If you are, then tomorrow I want you to be the opposite, even if they have to call the hospital and find you a psychiatrist. Throughout the day you will force—because you will not make the change all of a sudden—a cheerful and smiling attitude. You will be that person you have so much trouble being for one day.

After that adventure, when you get home, do the following exercise:

1) In the first box, you will write down what your life would be like if you were to keep up, every day, the behavior you want to change (in this case, a bad temper). Map out a final scenario for five years from now.

2) In the second box, write down what your life would be like if you maintained, every day, an attitude like the one you forced in the exercise (in this case, excessive sympathy). Map out a final scenario for five years from now.

3) Compare both results.

4) Choose the key words that represent change and stagnation that you find in both scenarios.

How would your life be if you keep that behavior you want to change?	What would your life be like if you kept up the same attitude as the one you forced?

Comparison	Words of change and words of stagnation

Words activate the biochemistry of our moods; we believe we have experienced the same emotions because we don't know how to describe the dozens of shades of color offered to us by the infinite range of the soul. We are often unable to interpret what is happening to us because we lack the correct definitions that would allow us to know what we are feeling at a given moment or, in other words, what label to put on what we are experiencing. Hence the importance of enriching our vocabulary.

The heart has intelligence independent of that of the brain. So much so that there is a field within neurocardiology dedicated to its intelligence. With more than 40,000 neurons, the heart makes thousands of biochemical connections. The fact that we make most of our decisions with our heart is something that was already known in ancient times—we even find explicit references to it in the Bible—but we have only now confirmed it scientifically. Therefore, we must take care of our heart and thoroughly examine what we allow into it, whether that be people or emotions.

Emotions are primitive and are born from an intangible world that is created not only in the mind, but also from the fruits that exist within the heart. Feelings are constructed when we learn to give them a value within a framework defined beforehand through language. This is how we distinguish an emotion that has become a feeling, then the challenge is to master these feelings and not allow them to come into being on the physical plane. Once we are able to define our emotions, it is easier to control them and subdue them through self-control.

How can we change if we struggle to define where we are and what we want to be? If we don't know how to express ourselves emotionally, it will lead us to our mental ruin and, above all, to our inability to establish efficient communication with the people we want to help, to understand where they are, and to give them the encouragement they need to move forward. Even this depends on the amplitude of your vocabulary.

Train, read, and study, and your life will change.

WHO ARE YOU?

Let me repeat the question: Who are you? Are you well read? I'm not saying *how* are you, I'm saying *who* are you. Your identity is something extremely valuable; that's why if we don't know who we are, we won't know where we're going either. If you are battling low self-esteem or an inferiority complex, and you can't define it, you will have a hard time breaking out of the situation.

No matter how much you promise to improve, in the end you will stagnate if you don't start making changes at the root level. You will work hard, you will promise progress, but if you don't strengthen the foundations that support you, you will give up. You will be like an old house, which, no matter how much you renovate it, will collapse if you keep the foundation as is. You need to build new foundations, but you shouldn't blame yourself for doing it. You have to face up to the truth about yourself with humility. Rebuilding your foundations is a complex process: the truth will set us free, but first it will make us uncomfortable, it will hurt.

All change involves some kind of loss, we fear change even when we know that if we don't, further anguish will await us. Many people build their personality around their flaws and defend themselves by saying: "That's just the way I am, and that's the way I'll always be." They do not want to stop being "like that", because if you remove these habits, the stage would collapse and they would find themselves on the stage of their own reality with no role to play. That moment of vulnerable rawness is often devastating, but it is right there where we

EVERY DAY I TAKE THE RISK OF BEING HAPPY.

acquire the freedom to be the protagonists of our lives. Without the scenery there is no choice but to stop acting and start being.

Unlearn to be "like that", detach and evolve, readapt and flourish. Get rid of the habits that curse you, that store up junk in your mind and spirit. Get rid of what doesn't define you and treasure only what takes you to a new level.

You can always be better. It's all a matter of being determined to take on a new conviction and raise your standards.

Dare to lose, because nothing you lose will be valuable and you will see how much you will end up gaining. That first step will be difficult, I'm telling you, but very soon everything will become very natural and you will never want to stop.

Chapter 12

PhDs, but uneducated

Reading books is becoming the
only thing in the house
that you can enjoy in peace and quiet.
Julio Cortázar

E xercising effective leadership requires training, but this should not only come from the leader, who should be the first in line to be trained. Training should not be limited to conventional education, but should also be performed by those who want to change the world and promote continuous preparation across all aspects of leadership.

Preparation should not be confused with education in the strict sense of the word. Although finishing your degree, taking courses, and starting advanced studies are essential to your growth process, they are not enough to get you to the point you want to be: necessary, yes, but they are not enough.

Although it takes an enormous effort to get a university degree, it is still more common to find diplomas hanging on walls than it is to find education in brains. We were all convinced that degrees, master's degrees and doctorates were a guarantee of life skills. It is important to have knowledge; there is no doubt that being educated is an invaluable asset, but to believe that a degree is enough to lead us to prosperity is an absurdity.

You don't acquire skills through theory; that would be like learning the menu of a restaurant by heart to stave off hunger.

Habits, attitudes, the way we face conflicts, the willingness to help others, self-esteem, resilience, spiritual enrichment, and love are fundamental cornerstones without which a degree is nothing more than a piece of paper. It is this combination that allows us to become unbreakable.

Every day we come across wise people with no formal education and uneducated people with PhDs. There are people who have learned how to design a bridge, but don't even know how to say "good morning", others who can decipher the enigmas of the stock market, but don't know the value of "please" and "thank you". How you treat a waiter says more about your education than all your degrees and courses combined; how much you tip for good service says more about your wealth than the color of your credit card.

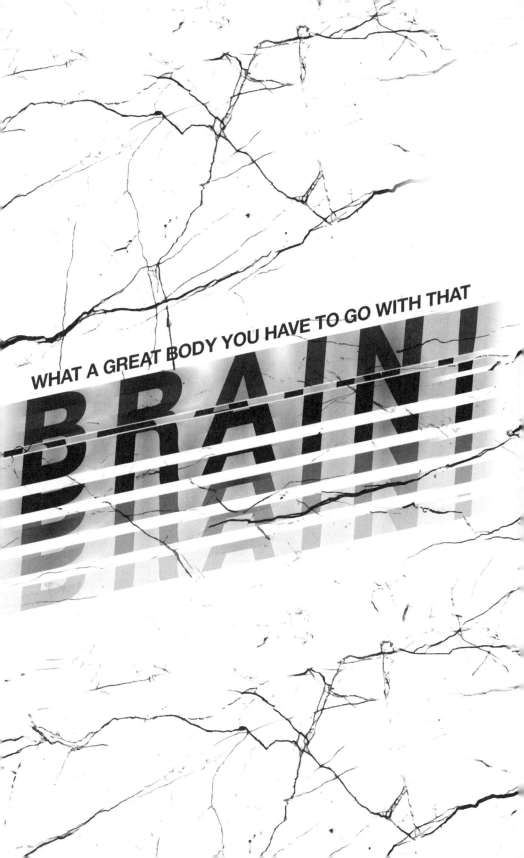

WHAT A GREAT BODY YOU HAVE TO GO WITH THAT

BRAIN!

Degrees say a lot, but do very little. Every one of us, from our own trenches, must push for change in the education system of our countries so that curricula include, along with the degree, education. Our colleges and universities deliver incomplete products: bosses who are not leaders, teachers who are not mentors, professionals who are not entrepreneurs, students who are not studious, and graduates who have not been given the freedom to dream.

Comprehensive education should be the rock on which a fulfilled, prosperous, and transcendent nation is built. Of course, theory is fundamental for technical and economic development, but it must be comprehensive if we also want human, mental, and spiritual progress, which is not to be confused with religious progress. We still educate our young people for a world that ceased to exist many years ago.

We have an educational system that delivers yesterday's tools to build tomorrow's entities. Knowledge is not understanding, reciting books word for word is reflective of good memory, not of intelligence, not of astuteness or skill.

Our students are taught to excel in math and fail in anxiety. None of our countries dedicates complete courses for the development of emotional intelligence, critical thinking, resilience, conflict management, body language, or discernment in their overall plans.

If education systems do not step up, it is up to us to move forward without them. The unbreakable should be an example of personal education and an incentive for all the dimensions of human development. This is real leadership.

We need a country, a government, a school, a company that not only tells us how much we are worth, but also demonstrates it by actually teaching us how much we're worth. I can tell you a thousand times how much you're worth, but if you don't do anything with that value, I won't have helped you at all.

There is no point in mastering the theory if you don't have the emotional capacity to sustain it. If our countries invested in the development of essential life skills and attitudes, our continent would be leading the world. If we had the commitment to legislate for the promotion of civics in education, to encourage self-esteem, the development of systematized innovation processes, focus, vision, discipline, organization, and order, how far we would be from what we have become!

Nowadays, ignorance is an option. You define and decide for yourself how much you know, learn, and do. We are in the best period of the last 500 years of

Adults complain about *millennials*, but they were their leaders.

humanity in terms of access to information. Let's look to the future with expectation and resolve to use our full potential.

Emotional and spiritual education, combined with professional education, is the only way to end corruption, crime, poverty, the lack of choices, as well as other severe underlying problems. True success for me is when people die fulfilling their purpose. A successful person lives in conflict, endures rejection and mockery, and is willing to lose everything today in order to achieve what is coursing through their veins.

We must examine what is lacking in ourselves and the people whose lives we wish to enhance, and invest in that. We must remember that attention, passion, discipline, and readiness are luxury items, and all of them come completely free of charge.

The reason they are luxury items is because they produce wealth. Material wealth is a consequence of spiritual abundance. I want to talk to you about the second one. I am not one of those who subscribe to false humility, the nonsense that asserts that you cannot enjoy the benefits of economic resources if you pursue a spiritual life.

I subscribe to precisely the opposite view: to have material wealth you need spiritual wealth. People strive to be rich, but they have a poor mentality and a broken spirit, which are incompatible with wealth. To start with, we are the children of a King, so what does that make us? Therefore, we are heirs of His kingdom. That is why we cannot live as beggars in heart, spirit, and mind.

Today I cheated on my cell phone: I read a book.

Immediacy is one of the afflictions of our education. We give too much importance to obtaining degrees, to making a fortune, to milking businesses, we don't stop, not even for a moment, to solidify the foundations that would take us all the way there. For everything we want a shortcut, an immediate solution. We run around like headless chickens. We are in the era of immediacy, in which deep analysis and meditation on the important things have taken a back seat.

A large part of this immediacy resides in vanity, hence the cases of people who are well educated, but ill-mannered. We need to take a moment to stop and, once again, see clearly, and listen sensibly and peacefully. We need to read with serenity and mindfulness as a matter of urgency, it only takes a few seconds to realize that no one has the time, nor wants to make the time, to do anything with serenity and mindfulness.

Giving yourself space to reflect does not mean that you lack persistence, nor does it mean that you put things off until later, it's just a way of assigning importance to what deserves it most.

Training and education are essential. Knowledge brings reasoning and reasoning brings progress to mankind. Worse yet, we are putting the emphasis in the wrong place, prioritizing knowledge over understanding, which is where true wisdom resides: know-how. It doesn't matter how much you know, what matters is how much you do.

We know how to conquer, but not colonize. We are teaching our young people to make an impact, but not to be transcendent. Our continent accumulates bitterness and pain, it sows ignorance and mediocrity, which in turn brings more bitterness and pain.

Failures don't only come from the educational system, the churches themselves have

Knowing is important, but it is much more important to know how something is done.

191

enormous shortcomings in how they approach God. You can know the Bible inside out, with all the dots and commas, but you can't do anything without understanding and revelation: one thing is what *they can tell you*. Their words and what *they mean are very different things*. We are beset by ignorance:

> The ignorance of our values as human beings, ignorance regarding our purpose, ignorance of priorities, ignorance of how to apply knowledge, ignorance of how to channel adversity, ignorance of not knowing what true success is, ignorance of not knowing that there is no such thing as failure, but the sensation of feeling like a failure, the ignorance of how to get up when we are down, the ignorance of having sight but lacking vision, the ignorance of thinking that education is only available in universities, the ignorance of ignoring libraries, none of them are threatening.

Don't worry about those extra pounds, worry about those extra brain cells.

There are thousands of educated people who remain in economic, emotional, and spiritual misery. The worst thing is that they have no idea what they are missing. They curse the fact that professionals like them have a bad time, but they don't notice the dryness of their treatment or the incompatibility of their attitudes with the world around them. They plunge themselves into regret because they feel entitled to a guaranteed joy just because they have completed some of the endless array of educational courses.

We need to take risks head-on, even if we only get halfway. Sooner or later we will find the strength we need to achieve the goal and light the fuse, after spending so much time in the dark searching for it.

Smart minds are willing to learn, but above all they are willing to unlearn and always keep their ears open to understanding. Learning without discipline is not an efficient way to learn, but learning through the systematic application of discipline makes you effective. If you also include honesty, you will discover extraordinary effectiveness.

I want to close this chapter with a really special task, one that I hope you will practice for the rest of your days.

For one week, don't go to bed without answering this question: "What did I learn today?" If you ask yourself "what will I learn today?" when you wake up, and make it a habit, you will see your standards of living rise with each passing moment. This will force you to find an answer that is so powerful that every day you will seek to learn more and, as a result, you will answer the question from a perspective of new knowledge.

But remember that knowledge is not learned by storing it up. You may "know" how to make an origami dragon, but until you start folding the paper with your hands, you won't have made any progress. Choose what you will learn, but focus on its application.

This feeling of advancement will bring excitement and a continuous competition. Put yourself in a position to achieve the daily goal of progress that will bring you untold happiness.

To start with, keep a record of what you have learned that week. If you can incorporate this habit enthusiastically, so much the better.

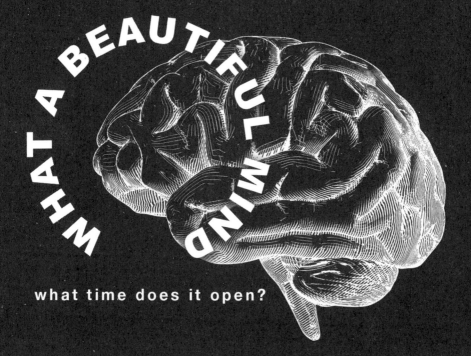

WHAT A BEAUTIFUL MIND

what time does it open?

Date	Learning	Date	First application

WHAT IS HAPPENING WITH EDUCATION?

I recently went to a work meeting and all the director wanted to do was to beat his competition as quickly as possible. This mentality is the result of a professional culture in which it is more important to beat the other person than to win your internal battle. This model is about to collapse.

I do not mean that the competitive model will collapse; on the contrary, competition stimulates productivity and, in addition, raises the overall standards of the industry as a whole. I believe that organizations that give away their full potential with the sole purpose of beating their competition end up missing huge opportunities when it comes to innovation, focusing their energy and putting their vision in the wrong place. The upshot of this thinking is not to exceed your standards or to create and grow opportunities, but to achieve a sterile victory that in the end could have dire results.

Companies should focus on improving society and generating value for all stakeholders (employees, shareholders, community, authorities, customers, suppliers, financiers, etc.) instead of prioritizing rivalries and letting reactive decision-making take over.

Today, the top CEOs of technology companies, graduates of the most prestigious universities on the planet, must be ready to compete with a 16-year-old who has a better vision of the future than they do. These leaders know that they must focus on winning the battle against themselves if they want to keep their organizations afloat. Without preparation, companies and

197

their employees would be wiped out in the blink of an eye. This training goes beyond the essential technical aspects; it is necessary to invest in fine-tuning our human wiring: innovation, critical thinking, spiritual dimension, neurolinguistics, and emotional intelligence.

We could make an endless list of companies that were the sacred cows of the world, firms with huge monopolies that lost their slice of the market in a matter of months, thus extinguishing the dreams of those who built them.

Numerous businesses were destroyed as their staff were preoccupied with competing against the wrong enemy: the most aggressive competitor was camouflaged by the decline in ethical standards, spiritual crisis, and internal problems. They stopped looking at people, and started to look at themselves. This has a huge bearing on the "crisis in the humanities," where the proportion of students enrolled in humanitarian careers is at historic lows. If we have been convinced for years that these professions will only guarantee economic ruin, then how could it be otherwise? Beginning at home with the family, any initiative on the part of young people to study philosophy or literature is looked upon with disdain.

Emotional and spiritual teaching has lost its attractiveness in recent years, despite the dramatic changes that have taken place in our society. Today, if you were to enroll in a calligraphy course, people would mock you for pursuing a humanistic interest, but at the same time they would consider themselves admirers of Steve Jobs for his great technological achievements.

We urgently need emotional and spiritual education to adapt to the new demands of society in the digital age. It is foolish to think that the humanities are not productive, especially on a continent where there is so much need to teach young people to express themselves, to use words and language in a positive and productive way. Linguistics not only shapes our minds, it is fundamental to the development of artificial intelligence and computer languages.

If we invested in innovation in the human sciences, we would be a new world all together. If we were to apply small but profound changes in teaching methodology in schools and homes, it would bring about a radical change. Degrees certify you to a company, not to life. It's highly likely that what you learned yesterday will be obsolete tomorrow.

Invention and reinvention are the primary essence of every creative endeavor and of every profound impact on history. I notice how in schools they teach the development of the creative spirit in a mechanical way, this is like using *software* to write poetry.

We need to understand that imagination is the ultimate expression of human freedom.

Chapter 13

An absurd world

I was receiving an endless flow of ideas,
and the hardest thing of all was to
grab them quickly enough.
Nikola Tesla

One quality that is often put on the back burner when it comes to group leadership is being able to think from new perspectives. Innovation must be a guiding principle, both in the spark ignited in the leader, and in the spark that the leader ignites in others to set fire to the established norm.

We have just touched on the issue of training, and all the implications this has for the kind of citizens and professionals our continent is hoping to develop in the coming decades.

In the previous chapter, our focus was on preparedness and education. In this chapter we will address the creative resources that the leader can bring to his team, his peers and his environment. We will also write about how to be creative. We mustn't forget that leadership doesn't just come from positions of power, but also from any platform that enables us to have a meaningful impact and influence.

The wisdom of the spirit is the most advanced technology available to human beings.

Wisdom is not the same as intelligence. Intelligence is the mental capacity to think quickly, to see the connections between things, to remember data, to analyze, and to envision.

Thousands of intelligent people lack wisdom. If you are successful at the wrong thing you failed as a successful person. The perfect example is that of serial killers, many of whom are intelligent, but not wise.

We also shouldn't confuse wisdom with cunning: being clever is not the same as being wise. Cunning will say that you can get away with a lie, but wisdom shows that truth is the only way to live freely. Cunning will tell you that you can do wrong without anyone noticing, but wisdom teaches us that there is always someone from whose gaze we cannot escape.

Humility is one of the paths that lead to wisdom. The opposite of humility is pride; the proud person only talks about himself, only cares about satisfying his own desires, demands that the world accepts his constructed reality and removes the perspective of the world we all see.

The job of a

DREAMER

is to imagine how to
reduce the suffering of

OTHERS.

From pride it is very difficult to see new perspectives, because greatness can only be achieved with a mind that is ready to receive and a spirit that is filled with instinct. However, in pride the mind is cluttered and the heart is empty. Wisdom opens doors that money cannot. Only the brave are able to rid themselves of pride, hatred, resentment, pain, and prejudice; this is only achieved by the courageous.

It is difficult to explore new ideas from a position of pride because we are overwhelmed with judgment of others.

Those who are afraid to dream the impossible ridicule others to gain a brief moment of attention; they offer unfounded opinions because they want to appear *cool* and interesting. When we develop new ideas, we must be prepared to be ridiculed by others who have disdain for new perspectives. These ideas don't originate as flawless, a majority will emerge with imperfections and inadequacies. This is precisely why these ideas are there, lying dormant and waiting for someone to bring them to bloom.

In the beginning, it is important to have the resilience to take these ideas to their full potential, even when they may seem flawed and lacking proper shape. You must be able to accept criticism from those who, by surrounding themselves with superficiality, feign sophistication. Place your ideas in the sun, water and prune them until, when the time comes, they are ready to bear fruit. That will be the time when you will have to share that consistent and sweet fruit with others, and return once again to sowing. Nurture your mind with the seed of the spirit and you will reap a harvest that is otherworldly.

You will recall that in Chapter 4 we talked about the importance of accumulating errors. We used to say that there are no silly ideas, that when great inventions are born they often make us doubt our sanity. Now we will go a step further to systematize how we can turn a far-fetched idea into one that is both novel and applicable.

No matter what field you work in, it is always necessary to have imagination. Never think that this is a dimension exclusive to poets, painters, or inventors. Creativity is applicable to all areas of your life, from relationships to establishing a new business.

Stupidity resides in the house of mockery.

The bad news for those who are lazy is that innovation requires hard work. Some describe creativity as a light that comes on, and while it may be the case that the spark comes from a stroke of inspiration or a passing epiphany, the unbreakable know that in 99% of cases, generating a new idea requires dedication and the utilization of cognitive strategies. In order for that light to come on, thousands of kilometers of power lines are required.

These connections are made up of several components: discipline in creation, observation and collection of relevant information, fearlessness in the face of what *people will say*, feedback, and persistence. I will stop at fearlessness in the face of criticism and what *people will say* because you must be alert to distinguish between a candid opinion and a vindictive one. Both appear to be quite similar in flavor, however, while the former acts as a harsh remedy, the latter will only serve to poison you.

Although your ideas may be valuable and highly creative, if you don't execute them well, you run the risk of getting crushed. The first step is to seize your opportunities, no matter how small they may seem. At times, if we are arrogant and anticipate only the big opportunities and grand ideas, we disregard the smaller things; only those who appreciate the little things will be rewarded with bigger opportunities.

> **Do not accept "constructive" criticism from those who have constructed nothing.**
>
> ✔

The small opens the door to the big: a small seed produces a tree, a tree produces a fruit, a fruit provides a juice, a juice engenders a product, a product gives rise to a company, a company forms a group, a group founds an empire, an empire cements an industry, an industry builds a community, a community creates a city, a city gives direction to a country, which together with other countries form continents, continents shape the planet, planets integrate a galaxy, a galaxy completes the cosmos, and so on to the point where reason loses validity.

Small is not small, take advantage of everything that it brings. A true leader sees past what is immediately obvious. Do the small things with care and precision, and pave the way for a successful future. The small can be immense.

You may never have thought of it this way, but creativity is an act of courage. Taking on creativity on a permanent basis is more than just sitting back and waiting for inspiration to strike. I say it is an act of courage because it requires discipline and great bravery to convince others that this small and imperfect plant will eventually become a sturdy tree capable of offering us shade.

To begin with, it is only the brave who are able to convince themselves. Subsequently, you would require a further dose of courage to assume repeated setbacks, as many times as necessary, as the process of transforming a conceptual design into a tangible creation is not always an easy task.

You must have the courage to accept the commitment to question everything, to sit and watch others, to spoil things, to always ask "why, why, why, why?", to imagine worlds and fantastic beings that do not yet exist. With all possible seriousness, have fun, find others who are ready to have fun with you, and look at things from an absurd perspective. In short, you are tasked with taking on a childlike demeanor.

Of all the terrifying things I mentioned in the previous paragraphs, none of them is as scary as taking the first step, which is, ultimately, the most important step of all.

The role of a dreamer is to create a more profound reality, conveying to the modern and twisted world that he and his dreams should not be messed with. To introduce innovative ideas, you have to look for unexpected connections. If I tell you that one of the keys is dissatisfaction, you'll think I'm crazy, and maybe you'll even tell me that you don't even want to write that in your book. I will explain.

Dissatisfaction lies at the heart of many solutions. There are devices that we have been using for years that have disadvantages that we don't think about and don't pay attention to. Dissatisfaction is a path in itself; many innovation groups use methods that are based on imagining things that don't work. Here are a few examples that come to mind: airplanes that don't fly, clothes that get destroyed in the wash, or watches that don't show the time. Choose one of these examples and imagine a product. I'm going to use the last example, watches that don't show the time, and work on that:

We must put an end to the dreadful habit of giving up for no reason.

This watch shows the months left to fulfill the goal I set for myself; the days left to see the person I love, the years left until my retirement. It may no longer be a regular watch, but it will be a new option for expanding the concept. Creativity is not always about creating or inventing: it can be about removing or reducing. What would happen if you removed chairs from a school classroom? What would happen if you reduced the size of a walking stick? Ask yourself the strangest questions you can imagine, because everything around you is a space that is worth questioning, and with it a space worthy of being improved. If we take the key points above, we go back to thinking like children, avoiding the fear of ridicule and having fun.

We could, then, come up with the idea of a watch that would show the unforgettable moments in our calendar: the happy days, the sad days, and thus perform a diagnosis of our life on a daily, monthly, or yearly basis.

Does it exist? Is it possible? Is it feasible? It will end up not being a watch, perhaps it will be an app that you can install on your phone or the precursor to a personal assistant. After that, we will probably even forget that misguided idea that gave rise to the idea and come up with something much better. Having nothing allows us to start with a blank slate, which holds endless possibilities for growth.

What we have just seen is the light that comes on, and behind it is the power line that we were talking about. If we are seeking a new concept for our cupcake or web design company, we need to be aware of the latest developments within that industry, we need to talk to customers, employees, and suppliers, we need to know our product and the products of our competitors, we need to know what is successful globally, from within our category, whatever it may be, right down to consumer staples, such as fashion, music, or entertainment. The rhythm of reggaeton or the latest fashion series may hold the inspiration we need. If we know what resonates in the hearts of our potential customers, we are much more likely to make effective connections.

Do a brief exercise to activate these connections:

1) Ask a person around you, even better if it's a customer, which of the fashionable songs he or she likes.
2) Ask them what their favorite TV series is.
3) Take elements from both answers and build up an imaginary world.
4) Design a product or service for the inhabitants of that imaginary world. It may be something totally absurd, but associated with your area of interest (e.g., the cupcake company).
5) Then take that imaginary product and connect it to something that exists in the real world.

Write the results here.

As you practice and make more complex connections, you will be able to activate your ingenuity and find all kinds of links.

As I said before, these exercises are not exclusive to those whose purpose is creation—artists, inventors, advertisers, or designers—everyone needs them because innovation is required across all spaces. Originality may emerge in the way you fall in love with that person, in how you prepare your projects or decorate your children's party, but it plays a much more important and necessary role when it comes to how you lead and help others.

We need to find ways to provide children and young people with tools that will help them change their perspectives. There is an urgent need to teach this type of tool at all educational levels, regardless of the field in question. Learning to think is a fundamental part of growth and continuous improvement.

Before continuing to conquer other planets or outer space, why don't we conquer inner space?

To innovate, we must ask the right questions. If we say: "How can I do this if it's impossible?" you won't even try to do it anymore, you've already condemned yourself to defeat. The answer is already implicit, it prevents the development of a fresh perspective and inhibits the exploration of different paths of understanding. In that place, the word "no" holds more power than the benefit of the doubt, and the idea of faith transforms into something intangible. It's better to ask yourself: "How do I make it possible?" And then respond with "Maybe I can make it happen"!

By rephrasing the question, you uncover boundless possibilities and opportunities, sparking belief and transforming

I MATURED:

I'm finally a *kid* again.

the notion from theoretical to tangible, making room for the actualization of the intent, that is, that the "yes" starts to emerge, followed by a sense of "maybe", and your mind kicks into gear.

It may seem dumb and simplistic, but we tend to shape our minds with the thoughts that generate the least amount of conflict. We should abandon logic, or at least reserve its use for occasions when we need to discern the fruits of our imagination.

MANY IDEAS

There are many ideas that you can think of, but not believe in. An idea is useless if you don't believe in it deeply. Whoever tries to manifest ideas without the firm conviction that he will do everything to achieve them, is only wasting their time. To believe in an idea requires assuming it as an act of emotional and spiritual certainty, there is no middle ground.

In the absence of certainty, doubts will appear, and with them your actions will lack stability and your steps will lose direction. Without resolve and direction there is no focus, and without focus there is no vision; without vision, the possibility of a significant change that protects you with an unshakeable sense of security that even death cannot shake, vanishes.

The will of the human being, when supported by conviction, does not waver.

With deep belief, faith ceases to be an illusion, or a mere concept, and becomes a living truth. This level of certainty offers the ability to surpass boundaries and imagine limitless possibilities, akin to unlocking the barriers that hold back a boundless well of creativity and innovation.

The unbreakable have dreams so big that they can crack marble and chip diamonds. Dream! And then sweat. You must persist until you achieve your goal, but first you have to believe that you are going to achieve it.

Don't stop, keep going until what you dreamed of becomes a reality.

But first, believe.

Chapter 14

Red numbers

Every fool confuses value and price.

Antonio Machado

know that sometimes, as we write about pursuing our dreams, innovation, transformation, entrepreneurship, quitting what's holding you back, or starting our own business, you've wondered how you're going to pay the bills in the meantime.

It is precisely for this reason that I would like us to dedicate this space to talking about money, and I hope that this will change something about the way you approach it. There are those who live to own money, not realizing that it is money that owns them.

Some people are so miserable, they save up money their entire lives, and never spend it. Making money is extremely easy, but maintaining a family, a marriage, a friendship, a healthy self-esteem will be the upcoming challenges of the millennium, you'll see!

Remaining detached does not mean that you possess nothing, it means that nothing possesses you.

Those who allow themselves to be driven by money are in serious trouble. The material turns life into an insatiable void that must be constantly filled immediately, it becomes the primary goal of existence, but sooner or later, it will cease to have any value at all.

Money does not make a barren mind flourish. The deep-rooted belief in the opposite is based on the mistaken idea that we so often hear at the dinner table from our parents and grandparents, who constantly repeat that the more you have, the happier you will be.

How much we are worth as people, and how much we are worth for what we have, are two different things. Things have a price, but value is not a number. You are a person who has values, that's why we say: "I live according to my values," and if they had a price tag, they wouldn't really be values.

In Chapter 6 you made a list of the time you spent on social media—not counting time spent on work—watching TV, or texting. It's time for you to look up those numbers so we can do some calculations.

Instead of thinking that the world has taken or stolen things from you, it's better to actually do the math. I will do a

LOSING
MONEY
IS JUST
LOSING
PAPER.

sample exercise and then you will do yours using the values that you define, in addition to the ones you carry over from Chapter 6. Calculate your part with absolute honesty, and brutal transparency.

How much money do you want to earn per month?

Here you will put a significant, but exaggerated, amount. It is not enough to want "a lot of money", you must define exactly how much money you want. Believe me, there is a very good reason for being so accurate. For round numbers, let's say USD10,000 not including irrelevant minor expenses. I will do the example in dollars, you do it in the currency of your choice and add as many zeros as you want.

USD10,000 per month.

Now, on that basis, calculate: if you work Monday through Saturday, in a normal month, that would be 26 working days. This would give us USD385 per day, if we round it up; but if you want to take two days off instead of one, you would have to earn USD454 per day.

For the time being, let's leave it at six days a week:

USD385 per day.

If you work eight hours a day, that would be:

USD48 per hour.

Now the interesting math starts: let's say USD10,000 is your medium-term goal, i.e., one to two years. Now let's add up the money you owe yourself and the money you will owe yourself if you continue to live the way you do. I am not going to downplay the learning curve or all the investment of time you have made in your life, because sooner or later that will yield its own return. The purpose of this exercise is to show how much you invest in what you think is free; I am talking about your unattained dreams. How much time have you spent on unproductive activities that you could have spent more effectively? How many times have you opted to go and have fun, play on the phone, or have a few drinks instead of doing the right things? How many times have you said "no" to yourself in order to say "yes" to everyone else?

If you wasted three hours today being angry, you owe yourself 3 × USD48 = USD144.

If you spent two hours on social media, you owe yourself USD96.

But if this is something you do on a daily basis you owe USD96 x 26, which is the number of days worked. You owe yourself USD2,496 for being on Instagram when you should have been doing something productive. Free?

Imagine if you also spend two hours watching television. At the end of the month you will owe yourself USD5,000, and you are the one who will pay that debt. Imagine how hard you have to work to pay it off, and to that you will have to add the time lost paying yourself what you owe, which is already generating interest.

Do you see how much you have lost?

With your attitude, you will have completely lowered your level of commitment, which means that you will no longer be able to deliver the same level of performance. You are the one who defrauds and steals from yourself. Add to your debt everything that has accumulated during all the days you have wasted being depressed, in a bad mood, afraid, and not trying to do what you are supposed to.

Carry over the results of the exercise in Chapter 6. You can do your calculations in the table on the next page. I will fill one out to show you:

How much you want to earn	$10,000	Days you will work per month	26
How much you earn per day	$385		
Hourly rate	$48.125	Hours per day	8
How much you invest in	Social media	2 hours	$2,503 / month
How much you invest in	Watching the television	3 hours	$3,754 / month
How much you invest in	Chatting	1.5 hours	$1,877 / month
How much you invest in			$8,134 / month
How much do you want to earn?		Days you will work per month	
How much do you earn per day?			
Hourly rate		Hours per day	
How much do you invest in			

How much do you invest in			
How much do you invest in			
How much do you invest in			
How much do you invest in			
How much do you invest in			
How much do you invest in			
How much you owe			

If you think the amount of time you spend on social media is exaggerated, open your Instagram, go to the settings and go to *your activity* and see how much time you spend on the app. You'll be surprised.

I don't want these numbers to cause you distress, but I want you to be able to ascertain whether this is what you want, and whether this is how you think you will get it. You can buy an airplane or rent one for a fraction of the price. There are many ways to get the things you want.

After this little life equation, would you dare to say again that you have no money, do you really believe that someone took what is yours? You're a millionaire, you just don't know it!

Once you've done this, set out what you are going to sacrifice in order to achieve what you want. Draw up the strategy that you will use to reduce the time you waste doing "free" things, and fine-tune the plan that you will implement in order to focus on your goal. Finally, you need to take the first step, and don't accept any excuses. If you're going to go out and compete, it's to win.

This should not be the cause of any anxiety. You don't have to live a life of oppression either. What is important here is that you understand that leisure and fun, although essential, must be in healthy balance with your accomplishments. In addition, you will understand that achieving your financial goals entails certain sacrifices, but never sacrifice yourself for them.

You can recuperate that money by being efficient. Just because you work all day without stopping doesn't mean you are using your time wisely. You won't earn more just by "working like a donkey". Productivity is the balance you achieve when your work and the effort you put into your life's purpose are in perfect equilibrium.

If you spend most of your time on something that is not bringing you closer to your dreams, I have to tell you, you are throwing thousands and thousands of dollars down the drain, it's as simple as that.

They say that time is money, but no, time has no price, it has value, a value that no currency can buy, an amount that no one can ever pay you. How much would you charge for an extra minute of your life, for a leg? or for an eye? That's the value you have.

Stop throwing your whole life in the garbage when you should throw all the garbage out of your life.

Time is not money, let's stop saying that. Time is priceless because if it were money, our existence would be extremely cheap. It's time to thoroughly comprehend that time is priceless, there is no amount, no number, no check, no transfer that can pay for a single second of our life. Let's understand now, this second that has just passed is not coming back...

nor this one...

nor this one...

nor this one..

If time had a price, a millionaire could just write you a check for every second of your life.

✅

Don't put your life in the red: it's time to come to your senses and stop investing in things that extinguish the flame from which your passions burn. Economic prosperity is a consequence: enrichment is not an end, it is a means that, if misguided, can be devastating.

There is nothing wrong with money, the problem is that we treat it as if it were priceless. By focusing excessively on money we end up undervaluing the thing that really is priceless. The more things we have the less we value them.

Therefore, if we align our actions with our innermost core, we will embrace the fundamental principles of our being and never again place a price on the priceless. Wealth is only born from the flow of the spirit. To be prosperous is to be abundant in everything: in mind, heart, and soul.

As we said before, it doesn't require great intelligence to make a fortune, it requires great wisdom.

You don't need to give your work away for free either. If for strategic reasons you want to lower your price, that's fine, but always do it within the framework of maximizing the fruit of your labor, and never to the detriment of your partners. In any business partnership, it is important to remember that if only one party benefits, there will not be a second party for very long.

"Daniel, there are people who charge me less than you," he told me, using it as his only negotiation point.

"My man, I can imagine, no doubt, but I also have people who pay me more than you pay me," was my only response.

In my case, I accept business and do work for free; I gladly offer my talents to causes that are dear to my soul, and I do so because I want to sow and to serve.

The worker deserves his pay. I do not accept that anyone should try to equate me with their pricing criteria as if I were the sole individual who holds the standard for determining everything. Who else is able to put a value on my time and my work?

If you're mind is poor, money won't make you rich.

You may perceive some arrogance in this, but it isn't arrogance. We are not numbers or statistics; if we were paid according to time, nobody would have the money to pay us for even one minute of our lives. We charge for what we do, what we know, and what we achieve.

There are services that are tangible, but there are also intangible services that sustain everything around us.

When you know your priorities and your value, you never go hungry. Don't negotiate when you're hungry, because you'll always be left with the crumbs.

You should not undercharge, but you should always over-deliver. And not only to your customers, but also to your employees and, if you don't have employees, to the people who work with you. Creating a good climate and fostering harmony in companies and businesses is a fundamental part of success. This prosperity does not come without cost. This aspect, together with the two points discussed in the previous chapters—training and innovation—is the only possible salvation in an increasingly fast-paced and fierce market.

The business world has reduced the human essence, making us numbers rather than individuals. A manager who relies on information from a screen to make decisions is already on track to losing their true identity as a leader, and is neglecting the

Once you know how much you're worth, you stop giving people discounts.

core principles of leadership in favor of outdated beliefs that prioritize data over individuals. Only when we reverse this order, will we begin to change the world.

Cutting costs for the sake of revenue by reducing quality is the death knell of your business. I promise you one thing: quality comes before utility.

Don't waste any more money: pay yourself what you're owed, start paying yourself and invest in things that are eternal. Stop making withdrawals from the spiritual world.

Start minimizing your faults and elevating your virtues. Pay yourself what you owe, stop engaging in self-sabotage, keep walking forward, even if it's at a slow pace.

Expensive clothes
don't take away the

CHEAPNESS

of the product.

UNBRKBL

A COMPANY NEVER...

A company should never sacrifice the heart and spirit of its people, much less their dignity. The highest standard should be ethics and the conviction to serve internally and externally.

Information triples every minute, and what we've learned becomes obsolete in the blink of an eye. Social, educational, and economic programs must be one step ahead of the daily transformation, but, above all, they need to have long-term application and vision. Short-term profits don't reflect success.

The young entrepreneur, the successful businessman, or the executive-level employee, when they achieve a standard and balance, end up believing that: "We're fine as we are" or "If it ain't broke, don't fix it." These expressions are a death sentence, injecting into companies a lethal serum against innovation, productivity, and effectiveness.

We should strive to have fewer and fewer people going out in search of a job in order to satisfy their immediate and primary needs. Our countries require a visionary culture of long-term project creation: we want tomorrow's companies, but we apply yesterday's tools.

Managers must assess how they will anticipate the needs of the local and global markets of tomorrow. They must identify and anticipate the challenges and problems of consumers who are becoming more and more connected.

It could be that the future needs of our companies will be to develop the professionalism of the passionate, which is always much easier than developing passion in the professionals.

Passionate people will be those who companies will seek to retain and consider as their top talent.

We will end up being educated on a global scale, and the battle will not be to have the best product or brand, but to hire and train the most passionate, dedicated, and committed people. Master's degrees and doctorates will lose their relevance. Facts and reputation will be the only important thing when it comes to reading a résumé.

We will see the birth of an ecosystem that exports and imports talent, one in which people will be signed or transferred, just as in sports. Companies around the world will hire and bid for people who will enhance company well-being.

I like the word *entrepreneurship*, and although it sounds slightly awkward, I prefer *super entrepreneurship*.

Chapter 15

Forgiveness or revenge

The weak can never forgive.
Forgiveness is an attribute of the strong.
Mahatma Gandhi

Together, we have already written two thirds of this book. In the remaining segment we will focus on human relationships. Many of the people who struggle to progress in their lives are stuck due to barriers such as bitterness, resentment, revenge, loss, or dealing with heartache.

Of all feelings, resentment is one of the most destructive; it keeps us anchored in the past when we should be working for the future.

It all starts with an annoyance that you kept bottled up, then it evolves into resentment and turns into bitterness; you end up being a slave to hatred, living in a state of embitterment, dreaming of escaping from the pain that stops you from breathing.

I'm sorry. Forgiveness is a gift to be given to yourself, it is for you, not for those who offended you. To forgive is not always to forget, it is to open up the windows and doors of true freedom. Forgiveness is an act of love for oneself, it is something that elevates you beyond the ordinary and brings you closer to God. Forgiveness is for sophisticated, brave, and wise people, never forget that.

Who is the person who caused this emotional pain and tested your compassion? Who bit your hand when you fed them, and then proceeded to walk all over you? Who has taken advantage of your time and affection like a run-down motel, taking your love and aspirations with them? Who crushed your aspirations and kept you shackled to their memory, stole your ideas and used them to become a millionaire? They're having fun while you're suffering. What are we going to do with him? What are you going to do? There are two ways to get rid of the pain: forgiveness or revenge.

Revenge is only sweet to the sick soul.

Revenge is as bitter as lemon, and burns at a low heat. It's a game of retaliation where there are no winners, only losers, because the wrong doesn't see the light of justice, even if it is avenged. True offenses cannot be settled, pain and injury

FORGIVENESS
is to be reconciled with your own peace

cannot be undone, punishing the guilty party does not undo the harm. Although it may bring you some temporary satisfaction, revenge takes you out of the world of grace and into the circular torment of retribution, where the wrongdoer will sooner or later be punished.

We believe there are only two ways: they pay or we punish them. But for me there is a third win-win option: forgiveness. Justice goes beyond just trying to even out wrongdoings, it involves more than just correcting mistakes and repaying debts, it also includes healing emotional wounds at a personal level by eliminating punishment and condemnation.

Forgiveness isn't about fixing what's broken or turning the page, but about starting a new chapter. Forgiveness brings a fresh start to your life. There is nothing older and more tedious than the terrible cycle of revenge.

Picture harnessing the intensity that revenge ignites in your mind and body as motivation toward achieving your dreams. You will notice the lively and innovative energy it produces, capable of inspiring you to achieve your aspirations. This world needs us to take the arduous path of forgiveness.

When we experience injustice, we first have to recognize that our perspective can often be skewed. If you are a victim and you take revenge, you become a victim twice over, first of the injustice and then of the pain that the revenge will leave you with.

Maybe you wonder why life helps and blesses those who have hurt you, and you expect fate to punish them. You will find nothing in asking and waiting for their defeat and their pain. Free yourself from the anchor that holds you back and keeps you fixated on negativity, grow, but do so authentically from the soul, concentrate on nurturing your inner spirit.

Through forgiveness, you punish them, expel them, you strike their names from your memory, and remove the marks that etch their names onto your body. By doing so, you are taking away the control that your tongue, mind, and heart had over you, effectively silencing the negativity and turning it into positivity.

I was able to beat you because I forgave you, and by doing this, I took away your power to hurt me.

There will always be time to slander as long as there are ears and hearts thirsty for revenge. But who doesn't remember the moments of their own evil, when you thought you were doing good? We have all been wrong, we all owe someone an apology, we have all contributed to injustice; the line that separates us from evil is in the divine trait of kindness and mercy. As spectators we cannot put an end to existing evil, but we can master the evil that arises within us. With that purity, we will turn to our accusers and say: "I bless you for having been in my life, and I hold you responsible for creating the bad that I turned into good. You also made me grow".

You can create something beautiful out of forgiveness, out of breaking a mental chain. Everything that happens to you is for the best. A wise person understands how to reverse evil, he doesn't waste a single second of his life handing over power to bitterness and hatred. Stop dwelling on your failures, leave before your resentment starts to pollute your own environment.

Forgiveness is the only thing that has the capacity to break the chains of injustice and give us the possibility of a future free of the past and full of new possibilities. Forgiveness is not an emotion, it is an act of will that does not depend on the feelings of the heart, but by the greatness of the spirit.

Resentment is a dagger that penetrates your soul and stifles any possibility of growth. Most people refuse to forgive because they believe that injustice will triumph if they do. This is not the case: retaliation is the opposite of truth. Forgiveness is a piece of the demanding discipline of love, it is the true path to freedom.

I realize that there are some atrocities in the face of which forgiveness would be absurd. However, even in extreme situations you will not find peace and joy in revenge, any more than you will find it in taking justice into your own hands. There are always paths and strategies that can lead you to get what you want without tainting your soul.

> **The challenge is not to let these people go, the challenge is to let go of the piece of you that stayed with them.**

Put an end once and for all to the vengeance that keeps you from moving forward, that leads you to run around in circles like a dog chasing its tail. So let's drive back madness with the sword of love, and let resentment and anger bow down before compassion.

When I have discussed this topic in some forums, the phrase "I forgive, but I don't forget" always comes up. No doubt, forgetting is one of the paths to forgiveness, but some situations cannot be forgotten. Forgiveness invites us to forget and to break with resentment and self-flagellation; forgiveness does not consist of temporary amnesia, on the contrary, it is a mechanism that allows you to explore your wounds and remember your pain from a perspective of kindness and mercy. In that way, you become elevated to a new level of wisdom and peace.

Forgiveness is a privilege that gives you the ability to see your suffering, not as something you wish to erase, but as something worth remembering and something to be proud of; it allows you to make it part of who you are, your identity, and to accept that this scar tells a great story about you.

When you forgive, the offense doesn't pass until you have assumed and paid the debt, knowing that it will be recorded as an asset on the balance sheet of your life as a human being. Swapping hatred for forgiveness pays a fortune and earns you interest, because every time you forgive you make a gesture that you yourself will need someday.

Search for the positives within the unimaginable calamity; with belief, you will discover them in unexpected places. Forgiving great offenses will never be cheap, it is an act of courage, evolution, and spiritual strength. Forgiveness is more than accepting the debt, it is assuming the injustice and the loss.

People who hurt us almost always bring us closer to God than those who love us. There are friends who also unwittingly harm us and become terrorists who are blinded by our cause. There are very few who challenge us to improve and confront us with the truth.

However, the individual causing you pain fails to recognize the impact their actions have on your vulnerable heart, instead choosing to further deepen the divide between you. I bless them, for when I became rich, they impoverished me; when I built a house, they destroyed my home; when I dreamed, they woke me up; when I became wise, they accused me of being a fool; when I lost everything, they took away my crumbs. I bless them because they worked for me without even realizing it, as they have allowed me to spend more time in reflection and discover the path for my own journey. Without enemies I wouldn't be writing this with you today. I bless them because all evil, when addressed in wisdom, works for good. My enemies taught me to appreciate what no one had ever seen in me; they were able to make me squeeze out every last drop of my goodness.

When love is your answer, the question will never matter.

Resentment is like a room full of nails. Never believe that you are weak for offering forgiveness, that it makes you foolish; never believe that withholding forgiveness makes you tough and strong. Forgiveness belongs to the wise and the brave, to warriors, to the smart, and to superior people. Whoever forgives is ahead of you in everything, because it is not an act for ordinary people, it is the preserve of the unbreakable.

I imagine that you can guess what activity I am going to suggest for this chapter. If you're thinking that I'm going to tell you to forgive the people who have hurt you, well, you're wrong. I'm not going to do that. I think we have already written so much together, and forgiving someone is such an intimate thing that I prefer you do it alone, when you close the book and I am gone. What I really want is for you to be thankful.

I will give you some examples:

I, Daniel, thank this person for bringing the best out in me.

I, Daniel, thank someone else for teaching me to forgive.

I, Daniel, thank another person for showing me that I am not going to die of love.

I, Daniel, thank another for showing me that I should first live myself.

I, Daniel, thank you, if you will, for bringing me closer to God.

Now it's your turn:

_I,_ ...., _thank_ ....
for ....

_I,_ ...., _thank_ ....
for ....

_I,_ ...., _thank_ ....
for ....

_I,_ ...., _thank_ ....
for ....

_I,_ ...., _thank_ ....
for ....

Are you brave enough to call them and tell them? Do it.

Are you brave enough to post it on your social media? So, I want to see your smile and the hashtag #ForgivenessIsStrength #Unbreakables.

Letting go of sadness, anger, and resentment, and turning them into kindness is an act of bravery. Forgiveness is a breath of fresh air that enters your heart. The cold darkness of

FORGIVENESS

is to be reconciled

with your own **peace**

the prison becomes illuminated with a flood of light. For the first time in a long time, you will feel at peace. It is the greatest gift you can give yourself.

Forgiveness and asking for forgiveness are the key to joy and freedom. I greatly respect those who dare to surrender their pain without fear of being judged or considered weak. Young people, forgive your parents. Heal those sores, release the part that still lingers in the suffering. There is always a better way to live, there is always something we can let go of. It's never too late to get in touch with the ones you love, never fear. Ask for forgiveness, and forgive, even if it is not given.

It's never too late to get your life back on track.

DISAPPOINTED

Relationships evolve, just as the people in them evolve. The phrase: "It's not like it used to be" is meaningless and has no place in our lexicon, because we need to be aware that people change, and we cannot expect someone to always behave or react the way we want them to.

There will always be someone who disappoints us, but we end up angry with ourselves for having believed. We ask ourselves questions such as: "Why did I do it if I knew this would happen?" or "How did I not see this coming?" We build up speculation and deny the undeniable, at the same time that we give the benefit of the doubt, and when they fail us, even though we know we were the ones at fault, we wonder: "Why me?"

It took us 15 seconds to realize that something was wrong, but it took us 15 years to accept it. Now my question is: "Why not you?", if you already knew, if you saw the signs, and the symptoms of that disease had already manifested. Your weakness made it impossible for you to stop the car that was about to hit you, and ultimately caused you to fall where you did. No one is more responsible than you for the good or bad decisions you make. Your growth comes from acknowledging that the only thing faster than the speed of light is the speed with which you make excuses.

It is better to win a soul than to win an argument, if you lose someone by winning, you lost twice. It is a tremendous challenge, one that is not at all easy to achieve. Banish from your life every day whatever keeps you from the mercy of love.

Lack of assertiveness and ignoring problems are like a GPS programmed to always lead us back to the same problems. We must abandon everything that steals our peace. It hurts, but we must accept that it all starts from us, from our foolishness or ignorance.

The fool repeats his mistakes, the wise man makes new ones.

Love will always be the best option. There will be times when you make mistakes, but always make up for them quickly. Your peace is priceless. You are responsible for your habits, your health, who you fall in love with, who you hire, who you associate with, who you believe in, and if you didn't make the best decisions, you have the option of improving everything through humility and wisdom, when new opportunities appear.

If someone disappointed you, let me tell you one thing: I understand how hard it can be to control your thoughts when anger and disappointment set in. Your vision becomes clouded, anger wells up, and thoughts of revenge start to take over. In those moments, we often seek instant gratification to ease our anger. However, the gentle spirit is the perfect cure: a humble prayer is so effective that it places your body in harmony, and so decisions are made according to the spirit, not emotion.

Try it, get out of that vicious cycle that keeps you awake at night looking for ways to make those who hurt you pay. It's a challenge, but you will learn to rise to the next level and master your character and identity. Little by little, everything that distresses and angers you will start to hurt less, forgive yourself for your mistakes, forgive yourself for having believed in them, and make a radical change in the way you conduct your life.

Chapter 16

Master redeemer

*He who suffers has no remedy
to kill the suffering.*
Pablo Neruda

Forgiveness is a big step in your life; it is a great demonstration of courage when facing the ravages of pain. It is one thing to heal the wounds, but quite another to tear off the scabs.

There are different ways of dealing with scars, welts, and sores: one is to look for sympathy or deference from others, the other is to remind ourselves of what we are. The first pertains to the external that diminishes our strength and leads us to place our essence in that which is foreign; the second aims to penetrate our innermost self in order for our life force to emanate from within and rejuvenate us, but despite enduring hardships, we remain unbreakable.

I don't flaunt my wounds, but I don't cover them up either. They exist within me, acting as integral components of my being, like my eyes and hands, my heart and smile, shaping my identity far more than restricting it.

I'm not going to ask you to walk down the street with a fake smile and a false grimace, but neither am I going to ask you not to have your moments for mourning and grieving. However, if you've been complaining for years, maybe it's enough just to appreciate that you're *alive*, and that should be enough to dispel any complaints you may have. Go back a few pages and put a price on your time, and you'll see all the money you've wasted on complaining.

Every complaint makes you poorer and every smile enriches you.

Being violently confronted by life can be overwhelming and exhausting, it may break your bones; but let's not be cowards and let's face up to fear, doubt, pain, criticism: that's where you prove what your spirit is made of, you'll see your character grow and you'll rise to a higher level.

There is no use crying and flailing in anguish. Sleep, tune out your anxiety, and rest, sometimes doing this is the best way to move forward quickly.

Speak only of victories and you will become your best ally. There are already enough enemies to overcome without assuming the duty of carrying out punishments. Live the

BURN AWAY YOUR PAIN

BURN AWAY YOUR PAIN
URN AWAY YOUR PAI
URN AWAY YOUR PAI
URN AWAY YOUR PAI

AND ITS FIRE
will provide light
and warmth to everyone.

triumph first in your mind, then in your heart, and finally make it a reality in your spirit. The only wars you win are the ones you plan; you can't reinvent yourself if you abandon yourself. Be content with the dreamers, the daring, and the brave. Get rid of the idea that nobody loves you, but above all, convince yourself that something good will happen today, that someone is thinking of you and wants to bless you.

Your fruits will be multiplied and the harvest so abundant that you will have to break down the walls of your cellars. First faith, then signs. God already has a perfect plan for you. He does not fail and does not arrive late.

They often hurt us so much that we want to speak up, say what they deserve and expose them to society. There are people to whom you give away your time, but in the end they just wanted to know the time. But it's not worth it, believe me, everyone has a version of events, let God's clock put everyone in their place, get them off the swing and let gravity do its job. Silence is for the wise.

Wait for the early rain that will bring you lush vegetation.

Hold every syllable and sound of your precious voice, and use them for that which blesses and resounds in the eternal, your mouth should be a spring of pearls not a river of waste.

My wounds belong to the most precious things. I have learned to love every tear, scratch, scrape, and betrayal; all anxiety, darkness, and bitterness; every grimace and every arrow. I learned to eat delicacies and leftovers alike, there were always difficult days when the pain was crippling, but in those times I learned to love myself.

For a while, I stopped paying so much attention to what others were saying and plunged into long conversations with myself. I restarted my walk from the inside out. I gave myself the opportunity to accept the word "no". At my age I know that I *don't* have to go where I *don't* want to and I don't have to stay where I *don't* want to be. I came to understand that nothing on earth lasts forever, but what you take care of lasts longer. I learned to accumulate assets, not money. I discovered that good times come from bad times; first I learned to love myself when I had nothing so that when I had everything I wouldn't forget.

If you see someone who is empty, fill them with love and not judgment, and you will do everyone a favor. In this world, you will embody everlasting chemistry, and when you take off your clothes, look at your reflection in the mirror without dwelling on your scars; instead, just accept that you have them, because you are the image of what you see: unbreakable.

Many are grateful for the gift of life. I imagine God wondering: "And when do they plan to open it?"

A moment of silence for all those passions you buried that have died along with the "I should have" and "I almost made it". Two minutes of silence for the kisses you didn't give and the laughs you kept silent, the "I love you's" you didn't say, and the hugs you didn't offer. Three minutes of silence for the desires that were exhausted by your fears. Four minutes of silence for the risks and battles you didn't take. Five minutes of silence for you to decide, change, and swear to yourself that you will never, ever again, keep a single minute of silence for a dead dream, for a silent "I love you", for a shelved risk, for a delayed hug, for a frustrated desire, for an "if only...", for an "if only I had..."

It's all about dying more times than you have felt alive, about being filled with scrapes and wounds; there are no small talents or gifts, only gifts that aren't applied with enough vigor. Hold fast, with the right attitude, and stay hungry, even when you're falling apart. Not one more minute of silence in your life.

Pain can nurture and uplift you in love, it can lead you to rebuild your inner being, and even compel you to redefine your purpose. Something useful and fertile always springs from pain if you let it; what you will never be able to profit from is self-pity. If you let yourself be thrown into that swamp and decide to pitch your tent there, you will have lost.

What hurts you is your reluctance to suffer: Don't be reluctant anymore, learn and confront, don't delay any longer what you know will come sooner or later. Self-pity is deadly and destructive, so lift up your head and carry on with your journey. Now is the time to say: "Enough is enough!" "It's over: I've cried enough." "To hell with mourning!" "Goodbye, I'm leaving this coffin."

Get out today. It won't be easy, but it will be worth it.

Your life is meant for taking the biggest professional risks that your mind can imagine; if you don't see it with your eyes, create it through your speech and do it with your hands. Conquer your soul by colonizing your spirit, and that way you will impose the will of the King. Take the first step and never stop. Stop thinking about what you will get and start thinking about who you will be when you stop complaining about everything, give it your all.

Die so many times, until you feel alive.

It's not about what you achieve, it's about who you become in spite of uncertainty and lack of assurance, in spite of your fears and poverty; what really matters is who you will be after enduring so much pain.

You will see this person in the mirror once you dare to make it all happen and give it your all.

Let go of the self-pity, it doesn't do you any good. Self-pity is sterile, sound your trumpet. Get up, go into battle, run the race, set your shelters ablaze. It doesn't matter where you get to, what matters is that you finish, that you reach the goal.

Very soon your tears will not be of suffering, but of someone who has overcome a crisis and is ready to receive a diploma of honor. Believe it and do it.

No one enjoys going through bad times or difficulties, but we can live through them filled with hope, knowing that God has a plan for us. He will always direct our efforts to our benefit. I believe that God gives us the opportunity to endure difficult situations as a way for us to alleviate other pains.

Pain becomes a master redeemer who has overcome the trial by fire. Suffering and betrayal are the tools that shape your blessings. Only if you manage to see it as a companion will you know how to support it, will you be able to lean on its teachings; otherwise it will only be a sterile emotion, a suffering from which nothing flourishes, a sorrow that only destroys.

The pain that builds is the pain that lifts you up and removes the bandages of self-pity. If you are suffering and not learning, you are just crying without changing. Don't let your heart become deaf, filled with pride. Others will see you and know that the light that shines in you is not fleeting, they will know that your strength is born of the spirit and that when you walk, you tear away the darkness of others just by your passing.

Balance out your sounds, get yourself in tune, don't allow laziness and selfishness to dominate your time; subdue them, and don't give life to your contaminated thoughts, and don't succumb to the drifting inertia of evil. Remove anger, bitterness, and self-pity from education.

When have you ever seen anything good come out of anger? Turn it into generosity and joy. Life is a joy, an adventure; walk on ahead in spite of the winds and storms, stop just having desires, and turn them into deep convictions. Resistance to suffering prevents you from seeing pain as a gift that strengthens your spirit.

These are not just words of motivation: they are a testimony and a warning. Dare to dwell in them. Remove the judgment from your mind, elevate yourself beyond the obvious and the self-evident. Remove the ordinary from your body, and embark on a lifestyle that is extraordinary.

The problem is not that you can't sleep, but that you run out of dreams. Take back your ability to dream. Take off your bandages, dry your tears, because that mist is obscuring your vision. Give yourself permission, no matter how old you are; give yourself permission, no matter how many times you've been wrong. Give yourself permission.

Use the pain to learn that you can dream again.

The following task is perhaps the most complex of all the ones we have done so far. This is an activity that you don't have to share, it's for you alone:

You're going to set aside time—it doesn't necessarily have to be now—to dedicate some space to yourself without any distractions. For no less than 15 minutes, and no more than 25 minutes, you are going to write about the thing that caused you so much pain. If you can time the exercise, that's even better.

I have found in life that the people I admire have suffered much more than I have.

✔

Write in your own handwriting. Do it whether it is natural for you to write correctly, with all periods and commas, or not. Don't worry about your writing, this exercise is completely personal and no one, believe me, no one is going to read it.

On the first day you will write yourself a letter, so it can be read by you. It's a letter that you will write to yourself now, and express how you feel about the situation.

On the second day you will write another letter, you will do it as if it had been written to you by the other person involved in the event. If it's regarding a loss, write it in the name of that person who has departed; if it's a betrayal or a scam, do the same. It could be someone for whom you feel immense love or deep resentment.

On the third day you will write a letter to be read by you, but you will write it as if you had already died and wanted to send yourself a message.

On the fourth day you will write the letter to be read by you, but you will write in it what you think God would say to you now.

Write freely, and don't be in a hurry to finish. When the time is up, just stop. Don't linger in pursuit of syntactic precision, grammatical accuracy, or poetic elegance in your writing, the only important thing is to express your own thoughts and emotions regarding the event that brought you so much pain.

On the fifth day you will take the letters, and without reading them, you will dispose of them in any way you choose. You will do this on your own and without distractions, taking as much time as you need.

This is an activity that helps you to connect with the situation, leading to a sense of release, allowing you to have more control over it. However, I don't want you to take your pain lightly, if you can't get through it, get help. Go to a specialist: there are some critical states that would put your life at risk and cause great harm to those around you. If you are unable to channel your pain, if you can't manage to make it flow, I want you to view it with the same concern as you would view any physical symptom in your body.

HAVING HOPE

IS A RESULT OF HAVING PURPOSE.

DON'T GIVE UP

If you are about to fall and are just waiting for the lethal blow, I have to tell you, you must try again. Even if you think it will do no good, I beg you, don't give up, because if you neglect your health, your body will stop responding and it will fail you, because if you neglect your soul and your spirit, everything else will collapse.

Fear not God, for faith turns mourning into dancing and ashes into diamonds.

Rest. Even if you don't understand, you will get it all back, because faith is living in hope. Faith is more than a concept, it is a way of life. It goes beyond a spiritual experience: faith is the antidote to all problems.

Activate that hope, activate it now. It doesn't matter if you feel like you have died in life. Just the desire alone will be enough to ignite the coals of your soul.

Stand firm and wait for joy and peace, which is reserved for those who finish the race.

Draw your sword, get back into the fighting spirit, be brave. No matter your age, whether you are 20, 30, 50, 60, or older, there is time to embrace wisdom and use it as armor.

Look at the beauty that surrounds you, listen to the music, cherish your loved ones, taste the elixir of life, breathe the fresh air that we only feel when we live in peace. Your being is full of grace.

I know you thought you had lost everything, but there are still battles to be won. Nothing is lost.

Just one minute before you go to the grave, you will have enough time to change the world and the entire universe.

Capisci?

Chapter 17

Are you someone others should become?

It matters not how strait the gate,
How charged with punishments the scroll,
I am the master of my fate,
I am the captain of my soul.
William Ernest Henley

M any of our anxieties come from our relationships with others: with our parents, relatives, co-workers and, of course, from our relationships with our partners, to whom we will dedicate a space of their own.

It is, to a large extent, our inability to understand others, their motivations and perspectives, that puts us in situations of conflict and pain. One of the worst things we do is to interpret what they expect from us, what they think of our behavior and the position they give us in their life.

We are all different. No matter how much governments try to achieve equality, we manage to remain different; even if ideologues pretend it is possible, it is not possible to unpick how the universe has been designed. Diversity is beautiful; and if we are not equal, it makes sense that our results and visions of life are not equal either. We are metaphysically different.

By incorporating different perspectives, it is possible to form one single horizon.

For some reason we belong to a society in which the success of others is penalized, when our response should be precisely the opposite. We should celebrate the talents of others, and not condemn them. When will we realize that the sum of our virtues makes us better? Value is added through collective progress. We should not ridicule or devalue those who achieve success. Find out who you are before you ask yourself why other people's lives are better than yours. The world does not change, but you can change the world that you live in. In that square meter where you walk, you are in charge, no one else.

We must all ask ourselves conscientiously, what it is that governs our lives. We all have something that guides us, and we must be very clear about who or what is the source of that

THOSE WHO ARE BITTER FEEL THE EMBRACE

HALF EMPTY.

#UNBREAKABLE

influence. We all need to know whether we are the ones in control of our destiny or whether someone else is in charge.

Are you constantly driven by fear? A problem? Anguish? There are lives that are ruled by drugs, by sex, by an emotion or a mistake. Many choose their path based on what other people think, even based on the opinions of people they don't even know, who have the audacity to tear them down from behind a screen.

There are people who chase the carrot of doubt or debt, money or power. What guides you? I have met hundreds of people whose lives are ruled by guilt. This is a terrible feeling, a tumor that you must remove. There are thousands of feelings and emotions that could potentially influence the direction of your life's journey. We live on the run. Sometimes we live in constant flight, we want to escape from our mistakes and we hide in the shame they have caused us: that is where guilt comes from.

Those who carry guilt are killed by their memories and allow their future to be controlled by their past; they punish themselves without realizing it. Guilt is unnecessary self-flagellation; in fact, by feeling guilt we seek to protect our ego and justify mistakes or a lack of self-control. But no one is worthy of judging you, so stop doing it to yourself.

Those who fail to overcome guilt open up the door to anger, and those who harbor guilt, sooner or later, explode. Do you know anyone who has turned guilt into anger? Whoever chooses this path becomes isolated, internalizes their suffering, manifests it in their actions, and eventually projects it onto others.

Analyze it: Has anything good ever happened to you during a fit of anger? Has anything extraordinary ever happened to you while you were feeling resentment? No, right?

It is possible that the person against whom you hold a grudge, or the one on whom you reflect your guilt, lives happily, and completely ignores your existence; it may be that they no longer even remember the experience that still pierces your soul. That person may sleep peacefully while inside you are raging; they take their steps toward the future and you annihilate your present by anchoring yourself to the past. If you live this way, if you have not disengaged from the pain: you have given it control of your destiny.

When you close a cycle, don't get caught inside it.

If you don't resolve your anger, if you let it build up, bitterness will turn you into one of those people who complain about everything: "it's too hot", "it's cold"; "it's raining", "it never rains". No reality is to their liking, everything makes them uncomfortable. Even if they try to hide it, the person who harbors anger suffers the most, and we must remember that the people around them also suffer greatly.

Being stubborn is more than just stubbornness, it is not wanting to evolve, not wanting to solve the conflicts that have been created with others. Harboring grief for the rest of your life is stupid. We think that suffering makes us martyrs, that it leads us to deserve glory because we have suffered so much. Does your pain make you feel important?

We claim that our sadness is virtuous, desiring acknowledgment from those we reveal it to, yet we fail to realize it is nothing but folly, pure and simple.

Let go of the bitterness. No matter what has happened to you, life is exciting. Whether you have been abandoned, betrayed, or had an arm cut off, you must leave bitterness behind, it is nothing more than dependence on others.

There is no better language than the truth. Although the truth is taboo today.

✦

Our behavior is often influenced more by our social circles than by the actual situations we find ourselves in. Learn to accept different opinions, but approach situations objectively, without accepting malice. I know you will say that this is really obvious, but it is not so easy to identify on a day-to-day basis. This is why you should never criticize someone behind their back, even if they have really bothered you. We must always show our faces, show transparency from the front and from the back: all rewards must be made in public and reprimands in private.

"Hey, Danny, I have to tell you something they just told me about you," he said, his eyes swelling with excitement.

"I'm not interested in what they told you about me, but why they felt so comfortable telling you," I replied, stopping him in his tracks.

I have respect for someone who criticizes me to my face, but not for someone who is all mouth behind my back and no balls in front of me. Sooner or later I face it with a smile because our blessings cause those with bad intentions to smile as well.

It's quite worrying how normal it is for people to go around demonstrating to others that they have such poison in their lives. It is sad how there are people who celebrate the defeats of others because they have not achieved success themselves.

Don't show your inner child to just anyone, especially not for it to be played with.

A friend stops the curse, and will never participate in a trial in absentia. Cut the fuse before the bomb explodes. Never take a lukewarm position. To our friends, and to everyone we interact with, we must say what we want to say to their face.

My mother says that there are two types of people in life: those who will donate a kidney without telling you, and those who will boast that they would, but when it comes to it, wouldn't break a nail for you. You must know how to identify them. No one lives by the opinions of others, but many people allow their fate to be determined by them. We listen to advice when it is harmful, but ignore it when it is beneficial. We focus more on negative gossip about others rather than their achievements.

When we judge others, we put them into boxes, we offer our ignorance as a final verdict. Take good care of your words, lest God serve them back to you. Many of us tend to worry too much about finding the mistakes and faults in others when we should be examining our own behavior. We think we know how to polish and perfect the lives, talents, and results of others; in fact, we are excellent at solving our boss's problems, but we don't solve our own. We are a mess.

Let's close our eyes to defects and open our hearts to virtues. Let's try not to be hasty in our judgments, to be silent when necessary and to speak up at the right time. Let's be firm when we need to be, but not let our words be destructive.

People who only hang around with people who approve of them don't have friends, they have cheerleaders.

Reputation is one thing, conscience is another. I'm only concerned with the second one. Let's look at people not as they are today, but as we can inspire them to be.

Let's be discerning and learn to identify what it is that's poisoning us. Months ago I asked God to remove my enemies from my life and it turns out that I was left without several of my friends. Let's abandon senseless rebellion.

Rebellion plays a powerful role in the evolution of humanity, it is usually charged with passion and anger; when we use it without purpose it becomes mere hypocrisy. It is a double-edged sword that, used unwisely, can turn you into a puff of smoke, filling you with form while emptying you of substance.

Unfounded turmoil is insolent, vain, frivolous, and predictable. It becomes easily diluted because it lacks the integrity that gives sustenance to insurrection and thus to real change. Being offended by everyone, just because we have decided to be, turns our actions into mechanical movements with no sense or effect.

We have to establish clear motivation, a belief, a conviction for which we are willing to give our lives. Rebellion requires order, discipline, strategy, focus, vision, and love. It is an effective, but above all proactive toolbox; it does not focus on the other, but on ourselves: it is not "us against them", it is *us against ourselves*.

Of course, it can sometimes be difficult to detach ourselves from what is going on around us. It is difficult to detach ourselves from some emotions and ignore certain attitudes. That's why we often make the wrong choice to toughen ourselves up, but the effect doesn't last long since our reactions end up showing just how thin-skinned we are.

The most incendiary rebellion does not come from violence, but from love.

Why do you use a heart of stone for armor if what hurts is inside? If you are quick to take offense it is because you are thin-skinned, and consequently very hard-hearted. Better to change the order: crocodile skin, kind heart. By doing so, you will stop feeling hurt and bitter about stupid things and you will no longer be offended by everything, thinking that the whole world is against you and that no one understands you.

Care about the world, not about what the world says about you. No one achieves success without others letting themselves down. Your drive makes mediocrity uncomfortable, and even more so when you raise the standard of what is considered to be good. I'm not asking you to deny the pain, that would be to deny your humanity. Always being offended is like standing on quicksand. Don't do what is expected of you by those who don't love you. Love them, bless them, and forget them. Nothing is more powerful than never mentioning their names again. In this life, what matters is *what you say*, not *what they say*.

When you adopt attitudes such as guilt, offense, and hollow rebellion, you place your fate in the hands of others. Let's do a test very similar to the one we did in Chapter 11:

Miracles follow a renewed mind.

In the box below, write what your life would be like if you could make all the decisions you want. Think about what would happen to you in 5 or 10 years' time, you decide.

Imagine a future where you can make all the decisions you desire starting today. What would that future look like for you?

I make all the decisions in my life.

And in _____ years my life will be like this:

Now think of someone you love very much; it can be your father, one of your siblings, or your partner, and then repeat the exercise. This time, that person is going to make all your decisions. What would that future look like? What would your life be like in five years if your mom made all your decisions for you?

_____

makes all the decisions in my life.

And in _____ years my life will be like this:

Let's move on to someone else. This time, choose someone you have rebelled against senselessly or a person about whom you feel guilt—some heartbreak, perhaps—and repeat the exercise.

makes all the decisions in my life.

And in _____ years my life will be like this:

Reality will never be so drastic, I want you to remember these results every time you feel you are handing over control of your future to someone other than yourself. If someone walked out of your life, tell them to go and not to linger around the door, because they'll be in the way.

If you are one of those people who prioritize social media, what others say, their comments, do this exercise as well, but this time it will be one of those characters from the digital ecosystem who will make the decisions for you and influence your life.

REMOVE

FROM YOURSELF
THE THINGS
YOU

UNBREAKABLE

DON'T LIKE

ABOUT
YOURSELF.

NO ONE POSTS THEIR FAILURES

Never look at the numbers thinking that you are one of them; don't get obsessed with the *likes*, because you are not a number, much less the transfiguration of a digital world. It really doesn't matter how many *likes* you get per day, or how noticeable your work is. Don't be obsessed with awards, recognition, or applause. Don't get bogged down in online criticism, or give any value to virtual relationships. Did you know that you are experiencing the collective anger of millions of people? We use words as if we were not responsible for them, as if they were not laden with consequences.

We have degraded human relationships, as if we didn't care about others. The *online* world allows thousands of otherwise shy people to be heard. The downside of this is that it can cause people to act without fear of consequences, leading them to behave in aggressive and merciless ways.

The digital community will always tell you that you are not enough: not good-looking enough, not beautiful enough, not smart enough, not talented enough. There is always someone who has more than you.

Many people end up comparing their lives in a cruel and absurd way, viewing their bodies through the distorted mirror of social media. Don't give these attitudes any room in your mind or heart. No one *posts* their *failures*, no one publishes their tears, or their fears. Success usually comes in the form of a liar and a tyrant; if you believe it everything will end up shackling you, it will paralyze you, and extinguish your will to be better. In fact, you will no longer want to dare, for fear of losing however much or little you have achieved.

Every day, our essence slips away from us as we become the abstraction of a number, of a statistic that now represents a version of what we are. Don't take this virtual world so seriously, just learn the rules and that's it, don't get lost in it. You are better off giving a *like* to your life.

Don't ever compare your life to any other showcase again.

An *online* relationship can never match a face-to-face encounter. Never.

Chapter 18

Like an intruder

Let him lead me to the banquet hall,
and let his banner over me be love.

Song of Songs 2:4

To not delve more deeply into couple relationships would be to leave our journey through human relationships unfinished. Whether or not you have someone by your side, whether they are the right one for you or not, the unbreakable must love as they are meant to live: without reservation, without fear, and without lies.

Love is the highest and deepest decision that you will ever make; it is the pinnacle of knowledge and understanding. It is the material manifestation of hope and the human essence. Love itself is the only act that really matters, everything else is purely trivial.

I believe that hell is that place where love does not exist. If I'm right, it will be much worse than what we have been told. Love is pure enchantment, don't ruin it with trickery or cheap words. Love's potion comes in different packaging, shades, and flavors, but its spell only works if you invoke it through commitment. Love

Love whenever you can, and the truth is, you always can.

requires sacrifice, meekness, humility and demands supreme ethics. It's not about you, or your own satisfaction, it's about the other.

In love there are covenants and guidelines; just as your parents established the rules in your home, whether they seem right or wrong, there are rules to be followed in love. Think for a moment, what would your life be without these rules, what would a company or a business be without order and discipline? No achievement is exempt from consequences and sacrifices. If you do it for others, it represents honor and dedication; if you do it only for yourself, it constitutes nothing more than pride.

If you don't make love about sacrifice, why would others be willing to lay down their lives for it?

Never reduce your love to a checklist of tasks to be accomplished; it is a mistake to believe that happiness is to be found in another person: true happiness resides within you, a gift from God, intended to be shared.

It is about that person being the one personally involved in your "what shall I wear today?", in your "where do you want to go?", it is about praying together, it is about being three: her, God, and you. It's about getting lost and finding yourself in her gaze, making her laugh and ending up captivated by her smile. It is about not wanting to change the other person, but that the other person, for that very

LOVE

is the driving force
of the universe.

reason, chooses to change everything for you anyway. In a sick world, it's about that person being your healer; it's about you losing so that you both win.

Many say that if you love something, you must let it go; I say that only a coward would let go of the one he loves. If you don't win over their love, at least you'll know that you gave your life for what's great.

I know many people who give themselves to a relationship unreservedly, don't feel that the commitment is reciprocated. In many cases they walk away, when they should be doing the opposite. If you are next to someone cold, the solution is simple: kiss them so much, hug them so much, and love them so much that you melt them. Fire cannot freeze, it burns as an internal combustion.

When you give expecting to receive, you become a slave to your emptiness.

We give because we have plenty inside; if you give expecting something in return, then you don't know how to give. So avoid the frustration of believing that others will do for you what you did for them. Don't regret doing good things for the wrong people, your reward is already recorded in the eternal. Love is the sole action and choice that holds value, it is the ultimate tool that transcends time and splits it in two, it is a weapon forged with a material that is indestructible.

Don't take my words as being gender-specific. When reading my words, don't attribute a gender to them; instead, associate them only with love. Go and capture that person, because often the right time comes when we are no longer around. Maintain perseverance, get used to the environment gradually, don't rush. Conquer her heart with the small touches and poems, but colonize her soul with facts and truths. Be like a child, but don't play with people's feelings, because feelings always win by cheating.

Let her know that she is like your most cherished song, and you love her so much that she brings music to your life; tell her that when she hurts, you also feel the pain, tell everyone how beautiful she is, so beautiful that even the rain is enchanted by her presence. Let her know how overwhelmed with emotion you feel when you think of her; tell her

Relationships are not about possessions, relationships are about giving.

that your love for her goes beyond words, and your soul belongs to her, and that if God allowed you to, you would give her your spirit. Express your love for her quietly, through soft words and playful gestures.

Remind her that you would commit a crime if it meant being locked up with her, that she stirs all your five senses and the sixth, which is life itself. Tell her that when you close your eyes, your chest pounds from how much you miss her. And if at the end of the road, one night, when you are old, you find her disheveled, make it clear in your heart that a smile from her fills your soul with joy. Be like an intruder who, instead of taking what isn't his, allows himself to be stolen by her.

Love is born of everything and destroys nothingness. Being the last person to enter someone's heart does not lessen your importance, it just means that those before you were not important enough to stay there. Some people look for a better soul mate to complete their missing half, you should focus on finding a whole that you make together.

Those who come together due to money will eventually be parted due to money. Those who come together due to sex, will eventually be parted due to sex.

✦

Love is of two parts, of the flesh and of the soul. You don't need to have sex with someone else to be unfaithful, when you start deleting messages, lying about calls, leaving out where and who you're with, you're already there. If you don't want to stay in a relationship, if you're not charmed by the person you share the sheets with, if you feel that they don't help you to grow and tremble, then leave. Show some humility and tell the truth: tell her you don't want to carry on, but don't prolong the false pretense. Don't sacrifice what matters by chasing after superficial qualities like physical appearance.

Infidelity is much worse when it fuels a desire for revenge: you engage in physical intimacy with someone only to hurt someone else. By doing this, you will only punish yourself. Ultimately, no one emerges victorious: the betrayer suffers, the betrayed suffer, and those who engage in relations with a betrayer will also face a similar fate.

You could be happy with your partner or be at peace without them. Likewise, you can be with someone and be deeply unhappy; maybe you are troubled by distress because of an empty space on one side of your bed. It could be that your partner has passed on from this world, that you have ended your relationship on the best possible terms, or in the most heartbreaking way; it wouldn't be unusual if you have lived through two or more of these situations in your life. Each case is completely different from the next, so there is no one-size-fits-all approach to how we should analyze them. But there is one thing that all these situations have in common: they all involve you.

Here I want us to do a simplified version of a slightly more complex exercise. On the next page, you will find the pieces with which you will construct the building of your life.

You have a foundation, four pillars and a roof. Name each of the following parts with the elements that you consider to be the basis and foundation of your daily life. You can choose, it doesn't matter what name you give them, as long as you feel they convey meaning to how you see your life: money, education, fun, family, work, sex, ethics...

Do it now.

Here is an example, but not one that is purely illustrative. I want you to use your own criteria to construct this building.

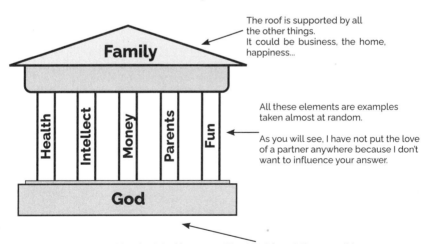

The roof is supported by all the other things. It could be business, the home, happiness...

All these elements are examples taken almost at random.

As you will see, I have not put the love of a partner anywhere because I don't want to influence your answer.

Here I put God because without that foundation everything collapses, but yours can be your own values, your beliefs, or your favorite team. This belongs to you. The important thing is that you can interpret them once you've finished. Of course, it can also be the love of a partner.

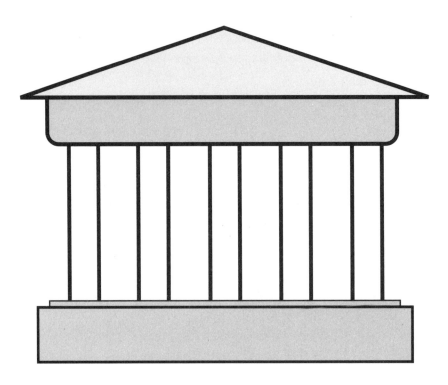

I want you to see where you have placed each element. Pay special attention to where you have placed the love of a partner. Is it the foundation of everything? Is it a pillar? Have you made it the roof?

In my case, the foundation bears the name of our Lord, because for me, without Him, everything would collapse. Have you put love of a partner as the foundation? So, what will happen to you if you experience a breakup or a loss? Have you made money the foundation? So, what will happen to the love at the top when there is no money?

If one of the pillars is missing, the roof will shake, but it will not collapse; but if the foundation is missing, there will be no roof or pillars. I put my faith in supporting the whole structure, but if you are not a believer, you can put your values, honesty, or personal mysticism there.

Look where you have put the love of a partner. What goes with it? What will be your support? Many people become dependent on their partner's love and collapse when it is no longer there. As a result, people either open the door up to anyone, hoping to rebuild their lives, or they stay in painful relationships.

If you want to make the exercise a little more complicated, put in a second floor. If you do this you must remember that at the top should be the things that have a price (e.g., house, tools, courses, etc.) and at the bottom should be the things that do not (e.g., attitudes, discipline, faith, etc.).

Those who spend their days alone—because they haven't found the right person, it didn't work out, or because God destined them to other plans—and those who have a partner in their life, understand who they should truly open their heart to and who they should not. Despite having this sixth sense, we still act foolishly and continue moving forward even when the warning signs are clearly flashing.

We are ambitious in all aspects of life, except when it comes to our feelings. We are often content with the little that someone offers us; we deceive ourselves into believing that this is love.

It's a big mistake to fall in love with love, before falling in love with the person. Pause, take a moment to reflect on whether your current emotions are genuine or just fleeting. Love is not an emotion or a feeling, it is an imperfect decision, and true love is perfected over time. Call me romantic, idealistic, dreamy, or ridiculous, but as far as I can see, these are the facts.

We feel the pressure of loneliness, and believe that it is better to be with someone no matter the cost. That is why we open the door to anyone who shows interest in us, who pushes us to take the bait, leading us into an emotional collapse because we don't have a firm foundation.

You will make a bad deal if you see love as a contract.

Some people fall in love a thousand times with the same person, when they take on different identities and personas. A night here, a night there, jumping from bed to bed, we eventually end up causing great damage to our souls, losing our faith in love, and getting caught up in a cycle of whatever keeps us going. A relationship that is built on something other than love and a shared commitment to creating a common goal is unlikely to withstand challenge.

In the previous chapter we talked about how we are able to surrender control over our lives. The same is true in the decisions we make regarding love: we feel the social pressure and we believe that it is better to be with someone, preferring to alleviate our impatience, rather than being alone and learning to love ourselves deeply.

They also tell us what the people we are supposed to love should be like. Patterns are imposed on us, and without us even knowing what they look like, we simply say yes or no to them when we see them. Of course, physical beauty is an attraction, no one denies that, but make sure it's a person you're looking for, not a list of attributes.

I adore my wife, I find her beautiful, my eyes get lost in her breasts, but I know very well that the day will come when that cleavage will no longer look the same: I also know that when that happens, she will still turn me on. Allow your mind to be your most captivating feature, and let your inner being be more alluring than your physical strength.

If
LO
VE
is your answer,

the
question
will never
matter.

Stay with the person who makes room for you in their life, because in the sack, anyone will do it for you.

If you have fallen into the same net a thousand times, why do you keep fishing in the same sea?

Depending on your bait, depending on your prey. It can be very challenging, because you are going against your habits of affection, but it will be easier to learn anew than to rip out your feelings.

Remember? They cheated, mistreated, and lied to you, or, they just left. You knew it was the wrong person, but you carried on regardless. Where were you searching? In which corner did they conquer you?

Recover your self-esteem and say "no" to those mistakes. Do not give up, strive to be the epitome of love. Take the risk: in love it is better to have your heart broken than to let it turn to stone because you run away.

THEY ROBBED ME

"I was robbed!" I shouted. When my chest opened up, the heart that had been beating for me suddenly leaped out and chased her like a ravenous dog. The robbery was committed by a woman with black hair, a pointed nose, petite in size yet as vast as the cosmos.

Our hearts communicated silently within her chest, making a pledge to always be there for one another, and to that promise they stayed true. This is the way it is, and will continue to be.

I no longer put up "Wanted" posters. I no longer pursue the robber because I know that it was not a robbery, but a celestial separation. I was made for her by God, and she was made by God for me.

I remember that nobody believed in our love, that they scoffed, they judged us, they looked at us strangely, they fired darts at us. But here we are, and they are not: Scripture tells us that "Each tree is recognized by its own fruit" (Luke 6:44).

I have lost some hair, but not the pleasure of hugging you. I have lost business, but not the joy of dedicating myself to you. I have lost pieces of skin, but I still remember the touch of your hands; I have drifted apart from friends, but your memories remain with me; I have missed flights, yet the skies where you carry me still remain. I have lost time, but not the hours in your arms; I have lost a lot, but with you I have gained everything, because I have you, and you love me.

My wife, you are my greatest success and greatest blessing, the more truths we speak about God, the more lies they will tell about us; but what does it matter if you, He, and I stand united. Let people keep their wealth, prestige, and acclaim, I see them attain success and renown, whoever they may be, in securing impressive titles, in claiming awards and accolades, whoever they may be, I see their accomplishments in the public sphere, but not in their personal lives.

What is life worth if you have no one to lose it for?

You don't need to win, but to lose everything for the other, that's why I insist that the world can have the world, because I prefer you.

Since I cannot love you more, it's like the butterflies that used to flutter in my stomach are now flying in my head. So, when they asked me about drugs, I told them about your smile.

So, I want you to know that it doesn't matter how big or small our home is, or how wide or narrow our room is, as long as we can look into each other's eyes, and know that infinity lies within our gaze.

Sex and love are not a test laboratory, they are not the result of trial and error. Love by losing yourself in God in such a way that whoever loves you has to ask Him how to conquer you. Revalue yourself, not just anyone should kiss your lips, not just anyone should touch your breast, not just anyone should undress your soul. Everyone, all of us, can be men, but few of us are gentlemen; many of us will be women, but not all of us will be ladies.

Gentlemen, before looking for an enchanted princess, make sure you are able to offer her a crown.

Ladies, before expecting a prince charming, make sure you have a heart that paints everything with color.

Love is not an exam that we have to pass, it is not a movie that we have to grade, it is not an audition to find dignity. Love knows no stereotypes, classes, or races. Love destroys all chains and fixes together all that is broken.

My wife, my shining star, my ray of sunshine, my friend, my lover, my partner; you are the one I want to be with today, tomorrow, and always. Thinking about infinity energizes me, you know why? Because it reminds me that we still have so far to go together. I love the springs, the falls, and the nights by your side, the pains are the glory of those of us who understand that we come to this world to love. You have made me love as God commands me to.

See how the sun lingers, refusing to set, so that I can continue to take in your beauty.

Choose to love someone who won't stray away; be drawn to their beliefs, values, and smiles. Love is a divine act, for what is united in heaven cannot be separated on earth.

Chapter 19

We learn life as we go

How can I offend you, when I only aim to appreciate the beauty around me rather than imposing on it my own views?

Juana Inés de la Cruz

The people with whom we share our existence are the ones who give it meaning. We are also here, in this world that has been bequeathed to us. It is something that we have to discover every day as if we had just arrived on the planet. The unbreakable live in appreciation of beauty. Life becomes more pleasurable when we learn how to decipher it.

Beauty is everywhere, crouching in the corners, waiting for you to appreciate it. Look in the mirror and discover how much beauty you can find in God's work.

If you dance with your heart, your feet will start to fly.

❂

It fascinates me to know myself, to know what I am made of inside and out, appreciating the details of my hands and why I have been given fingers. I always like to use my whole body, because everything I have, I have for a reason. I want to discover all the functions of my tongue, I want to probe all the rhythms and arrhythmias. I want to make firm strides, go slow, walk, jog, run, fly, and dance.

I want to have short hair, long hair, be bald, fat, and disheveled. I want to know how it feels to cry in the fall and what it's like to hug in the summer. I want to know what it is to kneel, and what it is to stand upright. My passion is everything I have, everything I am, everything I have been, and everything I will be. I want to live out all the adventures the world has in store for me. I want to learn and unlearn.

I am intrigued by my mind, and fascinated by yours. I am captivated by DNA, dopamine, oxytocin, pain, emotions, and fear. I like to swallow, to succumb to lactose intolerance, to defy the bacteria that insists on killing me, but still doesn't succeed. I like to trap myself, to hunt myself down and become captured, to be guarded and to be silent, to have moments of fury and to observe how it pushes aside my reason. I like to say sorry, to scream and explode.

I like to be uncomfortable, to feel alive, to feel passion. What a delight to know that I am unique and not a pale clone of others! What a virtue uniqueness is! How crazy it is to just be me! How wonderful

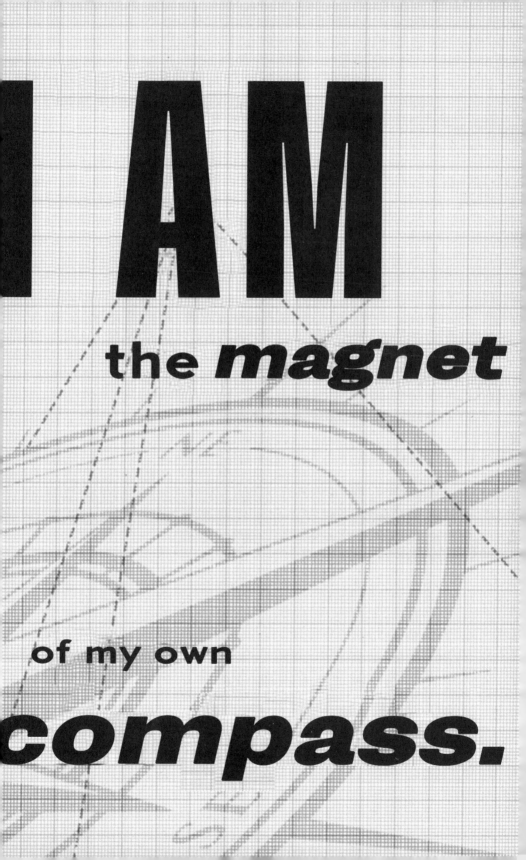

it is just to see you! Don't compare yourself, don't deform yourself either. You are incomparable!

Enjoy yourself and your surroundings. Give yourself some time alone. There are times in our lives when we have made so many mistakes that we don't even know which ones are ours and which ones aren't. We have accumulated so much debt with ourselves that we have no idea how to repay it, we hold ourselves to such high standards that our necks ache from straining so much.

Live, because life is often over before death arrives.

It's at these moments that I visit this unconditional friend, the most sincere of all our guides. I rest on her lap apologizing for the long periods when I forget that she's there waiting for me, faithful, ready to tell me what I haven't had the courage to listen to before.

We must lower the volume of the noise that surrounds us and hit the mute button so that we can find solitude, that inexhaustible wellspring of beauty in all of its nuances.

When I visited her home, I was unexpectedly haunted by a dream that seemed impossible, entering through the door of uncertainty. With the softness of her hands, I learned how to cut my umbilical cord, I discovered that it wasn't always necessary to have company in order to feel someone. Incredible things happen to us in solitude, experiences that lead us to think and pray. I confided in her like I rarely do with anyone else, her gentle voice encouraged me to express my inner thoughts, she inquired, suggested, and motivated me with her words. In the coolness of its shade, I questioned, rediscovered myself, and developed my critical thinking skills.

To ignore loneliness is to miss the opportunity to fully enjoy ourselves. Enveloped in its calm, the rebellion of ideas is born. Your silent bullet, your revolver. In its immensity, beauty is born in the form of questions, questions that are vital to our existence. In life you are taught to apologize, in solitude you learn to accept an apology.

Loneliness can also be a delightful place, but there are many who, instead of finding refuge in its quietness, feel trapped by the disappointments of the world, that come from expecting more from others than from themselves. Loneliness is one of life's classes, where very few get a good grade.

Don't be afraid of your heart being full of love. Not knowing how to love is not loneliness, it's desolation. Loneliness is not avoided, it's lived. It is a deep ocean of salvation, it is a decision that sharpens your ability to understand yourself and the beauty that surrounds you. It takes us to unexplored places of the soul, it helps us to rethink our values and convictions.

Loneliness doesn't change you, it just lets you know who you are.

When we close our eyes, we can explore the lonely and difficult parts of our mind and soul, live as an outsider, and, through the prison bars of our heart, observe how our thoughts come together and bring us amusement. Life provides us with so much beauty, so much to be seen.

How you view life defines the drive behind your gifts and talents:

If you see it as a race, you will appreciate its speed.

If you see it as a card game, you will appreciate its luck.

If you see it as a party, you will appreciate its enjoyment.

If you see it as a battle, your focus will be on winning.

A fleeting and impatient gaze can never be compared to one that is curious and profound. How can we pretend to understand and discern if we don't take the time to subtly step into the infinite power that lies right in front of our eyes? Few give themselves the opportunity to make time. We are a culture that exists through the constant and incalculable visual stimuli that, second by second, invade our minds and our souls. We must be careful what we feed our eyes with and how we nourish our spirit. Stop admiring what you don't have; we get used to desiring things from a hollow perspective, and we consider that our shortcomings are greater than our fullness.

There is so much beauty out there that we would have to live a thousand lives to see just one thousandth of it. The unbreakable go out in search of it because every day is an adventure.

When you wake up, kill that killer known as routine.

I am not a traveler, I am an adventurer. I am not a tourist on the journey of life, I did not come to see what others show me, I came to smell and eat as I choose, not as the *tour* guide says.

I travel without luggage, but I carry excess weight in my heart. Everything I need lies within me, that's why I travel not caring about where: whoever pursues only a destination without benefiting from the journey is nothing more than a passenger. I like going on trips that don't go according to plan, where things don't turn out the way we hoped or expected.

I like to swim out to where you can't see the shore, and climb until you lose sight of the ground. I have always felt addicted to travel, at first out of necessity, then out of curiosity and a desire to conquer. Whatever the journey, I always take on life as a fun adventure, a game.

I like being the visitor who visits his own home. I like the restlessness of leaving and the melancholy of returning. Traveling reaffirms that we all have to leave one day.

To travel it is not necessary to travel thousands of miles, you can even travel in the streets of your neighborhood, your city, or your local area. It's just a matter of changing your view to observe the environment with a new perspective, freeing yourself from the everyday to be overcome with wonder.

When I travel, I don't learn from the place, the place makes me learn from myself.

When your environment becomes ordinary and everyone always speaks the same language, sees, does, goes, or eats the same thing, you run the risk of falling asleep in a state of inertia, everything becomes mechanical. To travel, and to live as if on a journey, annihilates ignorance and uproots mediocrity, because wherever you hold your thoughts, you direct your steps. Many people say: "I'll travel", "next year", they keep planning, waiting for the right moment, but then they exchange the ticket for a whole range of excuses and forget that the right moment is now. I bought a ticket responding to the voice calling out for adventure and experiences.

Time is invaluable. The *kronos* is not yours, but you can influence the *kairós*: you cannot hold on to the minutes, but you can create the moments.

Look at the beauty around you. Those who are not surprised by the wonders of everyday life do not understand what life is about. In this segment, I want you to go out and see the

When will we learn that life is lived from the inside out?

beauty, to be a traveler in the scenery of your everyday life. How long has it been since you've been excited by the wonders of your city or your neighborhood?

I want you to get out there. Sit in the square in the park, take a picture of yourself with the icons you see every day, marvel at them. Perhaps you have passed by so many times that you haven't stopped to notice the beauty in the façades and the faces, in the corners and the markets. Have a coffee with the calm of someone in retirement and just watch the children play.

When you discover something beautiful, something that you have seen a thousand times without noticing its beauty, take a picture of it, as if it were the Eiffel Tower, the pyramid of Giza, or Big Ben, maybe its beauty will be even more precious and have more meaning for you. Wherever you are, in Chicago or LA, in Philadelphia or Seattle. Go and post a photo of yourself with the hashtag #GetOutAndLive #Unbreakables and then post a hashtag with the name of your city or neighborhood: #Miami, #SanDiego, #NYC.

Do it! Just do it. See how time passes you by like sand through the fingers of your left hand and like light through your right hand. There is so much beauty that gets lost. Blink and you're there, blink and you're gone.

Your home is also a paradise to be explored. The most beautiful thing about traveling is coming home and realizing that you no longer fit in the same box. Travel, we learn life as we go.

Build a reality from which you don't want to escape, one from which you don't need a vacation. On this journey you need to lose your suitcase, learn, but above all unlearn, get lost and then find yourself, look for answers and come back with more questions, get excited and then wake up, get drunk with nostalgia and laugh at the tears.

Become your own source of beauty. Let your face illuminate the journey of others. Darkness fears the light that emanates from the deep waters of pain. A smile not only illuminates, but also emits warmth, as it emanates from the combustion that burns up eternity. With your smile you can change reality and all its imperfections, it is a ray of light so powerful that it has the ability to give hope to a world that is ever more focused on its conveniences than on its convictions.

Smile despite your anxiety and sadness. Remind yourself that even if your mind struggles to comprehend the chaos, you possess the ability to make a strong impact with your words and actions that can bring light to the darkness. Smile for no reason, smile just because, just because you can and because you have a mouth, smile because you confuse evil and motivate good, smile because you lighten the burden of those who are overwhelmed.

Smile, even though you're broken, because you are grace and love. You are worthy of your smile. Trust me and you will understand, but start by smiling, your smile is a powerful weapon. Command your lips to break ranks and break the back of fear.

All battles are victories when they end in a smile.

Life is a personal assignment, you can't put it off any longer:

We value the house more than the home.
We value the land more than the feet that walk on it.
We value money more than the talents that produced it.
We value the gift more than the hands that deliver it.

THE UNBREAKABLES

Value beauty, which awaits you in the present: the fragrances of love, the caress of the rain, the flavors of your childhood, the intense blues, the joy of music. They are there, go get them.

I
like
to travel
while eating
in

PARKS AND ON BENCHES.

MUSE OF THE COSMOS

The Eternal One opened His heart, shook His hand and took the universe as a harp, marked time by thundering fingers, and you were born. You were born from everything, not from nothing.

The first sound pleased His ears, and, surprised, He smiled. In a dance He created the opera of the cosmos, gave it planets and spaces, stars and holes. Such was His joy that He made the earth and all its beings. He thought of the croaking of the toad, the singing of the birds, the rustling of the mountains, and the whispering of the owl.

Muse of the giant, voice of the cosmos, sword of the son you appease the spirit and expand it beyond the *kronos*, you enter the depths and dispel the shadows; your melodies are like thunder that obliterate the thorns of oblivion; the affirmations and agreements that occupy the emptiness; the musical notes that bring significance; the harmonies that make it rich and intricate, steady and unceasing. They give cadence and moisten the soil.

Wild sound, fierce roar. Everything is created and destroyed with nuances and flavors orchestrated by the soul. You blessed wind that tears through the instruments and spreads your harmony to the lost and the fallen. Don't stop, sound it louder and louder, sound it farther and farther, whether it's in a piano or an oboe, in the chords of Mozart or the voice of Callas, in the pain of Barber or the anger of Wagner.

Thank you. Thank you for counterpoint and waltz, for the *rock* and the metal, for the pure expression of a vowel in its unadorned form.

You are blessed because my heart exists to seek you, my ears to admire you, my soul to miss you, and my mind to create you. You are blessed, more blessed than the earth and its seas. You have elicited from me screams and frenzied excitement, laughter and frowns, uncertainties and feelings of being, insanity and serenity, joys and new beginnings; without you knowing it, I have given you everything. I could sing to you now and forever, accompanying you in times of conflict and to my wedding. At my funeral, we will take root in the eternal.

We will break the silence, and although not everything that breaks makes a noise, I think of the adagios, the rhapsodies, the *staccato*, and the silences. Even if the singer falls out of tune and the saxophone misses a note, the music still continues.

Everything has music. How much melody is there in an embrace and in a goodbye, in an "I love you" and in an "I hate you", in a moan and in an orgasm? We are music, the best symphony ever composed; without it the moon would only be a white sphere, love would be merely a hollow word, pain a tool of torture, caresses would be touches without meaning, waiting would be an annoyance, the butterflies in the stomach would be vomited and only my guts would be left, the bars would be empty, there would be no applause for the tenor, and laughter would be just a grimace.

How awful, how awful to think of your absence.

Without music, life would not be worth living.

Chapter 20

Unbreakable

When your will is God's will,
you will have your will.

Charles Spurgeon

T his book has long since come to its end. Even so, the three of us continue writing it together, yes, the three of us: You, God, and I, almost all the words have been chosen by Him, and He placed them in your hands.

I have left the last chapter to talk about God because for me He comes first. Although it has been present throughout the entire journey, I want to focus on His love that encapsulates everything. In His goodness we find strength, inspiration, and desire; from His splendor come our talents, will, and motivation; His grace offers us beauty, opportunities, and uniqueness. On this love we build our lives.

God gave us a purpose and leads us by the hand to achieve it. If you do not live in faith, you may find my references to the Creator excessive, but my intention is not to evangelize, it is not my place; I only want to leave a testimony of what this love has meant to me. This is not a chapter reserved for believers, nor are the previous ones, it is a proposal for the future for everyone. God is in the future, not in the past. He always speaks to you as what you will be, not as what you are. Believe it or not, today is an opportunity to look at your future from a different perspective. There are no mistakes before or after, only the mistakes of not trying the right thing in the moment.

Let's stop being yesterday's children and give birth to tomorrow.

If you wait for perfection in order to love God, you will never succeed in loving Him. Through my numerous failures, I have come to understand that satisfying your spiritual need is crucial in feeling fulfilled and complete. It is challenging to ignore this aspect of yourself, regardless of what you choose to label it as. If you truly sense it within you, its presence cannot be denied. The attempt to acquire material possessions will only lead to greater emptiness and expand the desolation within us.

You have the freedom to choose not to follow Him, a freedom that He has given to you. If you have chosen to move away from His protective presence but have still been able to achieve what seemed impossible through determination and effort, no doubt you have strong willpower, but you risk being consumed by a vortex of

If you are so **BRAVE**, *obey* GOD.

negativity that will lead to ongoing dissatisfaction and deepening anxiety.

I understand that you have believed for quite some time that you don't need to establish a spiritual foundation in your life. I also realize that there will come a time when, despite your best efforts, you won't be able to escape the necessity that led you to this point. Your steps will become heavier every day, because we have been created with an inner need that can only be filled in connection with the divine.

Following God is not easy, but it's much more difficult not to follow Him.

You may not know it, but in all those moments in which you have felt useless, in those situations in which you have thought that you don't deserve to live and that no one is waiting for you, you always had a place at His table. Whoever sits down to eat with Him, never rises the same: dwellers and executioners, the broken and the decayed, the proud and the wrathful, fools and liars, you and me. No matter how strong our faith or how many mistakes we make, there will always be a place for us to return to God's embrace, because what matters is not how long it takes to fail, but how promptly we seek forgiveness from Him.

Look up to the sky: if the heavens are so marvelous, imagine their Creator. If you don't believe, you lose nothing by giving yourself the chance to inquire. Embark on an individual journey, on a quest full of storms and tranquility.

God does not make scrap metal. He loves you when you are weak, when you are strong, when you are good, and when you are bad. He loves you when you talk to Him or when you keep silent, when you believe Him and when you don't, when you deny Him and when you yell at Him. God never changes, never hesitates, never contradicts Himself, never arrives late, never abandons you. Your life has a promising future.

I know that you have gone through circumstances that have remained engraved in you, pains that are not easy to forget. But add God into the equation and the result will be infinite: nothing can stop you, because He has not given you a spirit of cowardice, but of love, power, and self-control.

Look for it, but if you want to find it, search for it with love. If you want to know His true face, don't look for it in the face of the church, much less in mine; find His reflection in the Bible. God does not bless you for going to temples or prostrating yourself at altars, but for transforming His word into deeds.

You also won't discover it among the religious, who claim to distance themselves from society by labeling it as "secular," thinking that they are superior by bringing others down. They want to put God in a box, ignoring that God is God everywhere and that God is God for all of us.

They have shown us a god distorted by legalists and fanatics, they modify the essence and originality of the Word, transforming it into gospels that shift the focus away from Jesus and place themselves at the forefront.

To leave a mark on the earth, take a step into the eternal.

If you want to show what's in your heart, stop preaching and let your actions do the talking.

When a fanatic tells you that only they can reach God, remind them that it was the religious who put His Son on the cross. You're not going to change because someone *Bible bashes* you into "conversion".

No one has to become anything; faith is a way of life, it is a way of leading and following a perfect model in a completely imperfect world.

We lost the notion of providence, of the small immensities that take place around us. The miracle of life has become so commonplace to us now that we no longer even marvel at it. God does not need to set off fireworks or perform tricks: He filters the supernatural into the natural, the intangible into the tangible; His favorite game is to break the logic of our reasoning with treasures for us to discover.

We have all had that moment when, unexpectedly, you find yourself in complete harmony with your surroundings. Maybe it happened in the least expected place, maybe at a concert where thousands of people were jumping and you were silent while you felt the gravity of the moment; you held on to that melody with complete devotion, but suddenly, rationality intervened and pulled you back to the mirage we call reality.

God does not have to make noise to show that He is working for you. Silence is yet another one of His languages.

There is a way to feel that bliss most of our days, it is the adventure of living in the spirit: to discover that for certain moments, without seeking it or forcing it, we cease to walk in the finite world that binds us to our bodily chain, moments in which we let go and wander through the cosmos, in the stillness of the *kronos*, which has watched the birth and death of hundreds of stars swallowed up into black holes. That is the voice of the Designer of the eternal, the Architect of all that is visible and invisible, telling us: "I love you."

It is urgent that we stir up our powers of intuition, reconnect the mind with the heart, and let both be governed and directed by the dimension of the spirit, that powerful energy that arises from within us. The spirit takes you to those moments when you feel that you are part of the whole, that the cosmos is within you and you are within it; it causes you to look at what lies between thoughts and feelings, where the most profound aspects of existence reveal themselves and your gaze pierces the barrier between the physical and the spiritual. You take your front row seat to enjoy the meaning and purpose of life.

In seconds you receive answers to thousands of questions and you can clearly see the route that leads to the promised land. It's the feeling that doesn't invite you to think, but to act, it's an impulse that tells you it's time to finally call out to God. It is the mystical voice that warns you of physical and emotional dangers,

God will not do what you can't do, but what you don't want to do.

the inner compass that reveals hidden malice in someone's smile, the intuition that reveals jealousy, the instinct that identifies vulnerabilities, and the protector of your peace and happiness.

There are those who disdain faith as the naivety of desire. The worst thing is that many believers have made the same assumption. The connection with the divine is not asking to receive, it is giving without expecting anything in return. Our modern-day prejudices and the gross ignorance with which we view the Scriptures have led us to trivialize the truth and turn its journey into a few mythical stories, thus we fail to grasp the depth of its wisdom. Everything will change for the better the day you understand that life is about allowing God to use you for His purposes, and not you using Him for yours.

He who requests little from God, relies heavily on man; therefore, the challenge I will assign to you in this chapter is to pray.

In order to learn how to pray effectively, you need to learn how to pray. Later on, I will show you the steps you need to follow to engage in the most appropriate form of prayer. I need you to read these instructions carefully and incorporate them into your daily life. Follow them to the letter because there is no more effective way to get started in prayer than the following:

These are the steps:

1. Pray

Ready.

Don't ask in a vague and confused way. God responds to what is clear and forceful and nothing is more so than your actions. You are blind, but yet all you ask for is a cane. Then you complain that you receive too little.

When I pray—when I walk, when I run, when I kneel, during a conversation, when I cry, when I laugh, and in a thousand other ways—I open the door to the supernatural, to a world that we usually enter kneeling down and leave standing up, ready to fly. It is possible to pray in a simple and straightforward way, without using grandiose words. You can ask quick and effective questions, and His voice gives you the answer. He takes me and brings me back in an instant, and when I open my eyes I have a smile etched on my face that only the Lord could cast. For us to receive this information clearly, we must clear our mind of cobwebs and interferences, which only prevent communication from flowing.

Even if they cut off your legs, Jesus is the way. When the world screams at you: "You are nobody," He shouts at you: "You are my beloved son," and that must be enough for you.

My religion is to love everyone, to judge no one; to forgive everyone, to lie to no one; it is to dream that I can diminish suffering, it is to exhort love, to reconcile science with the spirit, and reason with the heart. Striving to resemble Jesus in a world that is different from Him is a continuous challenge.

I like to think that I haven't loved enough, that I haven't kissed enough; so I love and kiss more. I love whoever is in front of me and I embrace whoever will let me, because in the end a little piece of them remains with me and they with a little piece of me. Isn't this the only way to live a little longer on this earth, even after having gone to the grave? I want to touch, kiss, and offer words

We are not saints or perfect, we are unbreakable.

of encouragement. Here, there, everywhere. Face-to-face, I seek to fulfill my purpose, to build a legacy, not just an inheritance.

I don't aim to motivate, I want to inspire. I enjoy being crazy and seeking therapy that is unique to me. I don't conform to others' expectations, I break the mold they try to impose on me. No one is any less, we are all dirty, broken, or bruised, but what is fixed from above is always better, because God's love is perfected in weakness.

Seek to be upright and gentle in spirit, so that before you go out to change the world, you can change the world that exists within your own four walls.

IF GOD
enters the story,
the ending will be
PERFECT.

#UNBREAKABLE

CHALLENGE ME

I get angry, and He tells me: "Sorry."

I want safety, and He promises me nothing.

I am afraid, and He tells me to: "Follow."

I want peace of mind, and He makes me restless.

I hesitate, and He tells me to: "Trust."

I want to grow up and He treats me as a child.

I seek riches, and He says to me to: "Become detached."

I want to shine, and He asks me to pray in private.

I make plans, and He tells me to: "Abandon them."

I want to be a boss, and He sends me out to serve.

I am distressed, and He says to me: "Be calm."

I want to hide, and He rescues me.

I speak of peace, and He says to me: "Shoot."

I want to command, and He makes me obey.

I draw my sword, and He says to me: "Surrender."

I want heaven, and He throws me down to earth.

I think I am good, and He tells me: "Improve".

I want to return, and He leaves me in the diaspora.

I lay down to sleep, and He says to me: "Wake up."

I want clarity, and He writes in metaphors.

I always read about and witness a Jesus who moves around, who travels, who boards boats, who walks down mountains, who enters homes, who exits temples, who communicates in public places; a Jesus who purifies and cures, a Jesus who did not wait for tomorrow. I always read about an active, passionate, focused, willing, orderly, positive Jesus, who has a map and a route marked on it. I have never come across a portrayal of Jesus as passive, unresponsive, dull, motionless, or much less lazy.

Jairus sought Jesus in despair; his daughter had died; he asked him to come to him, told him what he thought he needed and declared in faith: there is a faith in resurrection that exists only when even after death you speak as if everything were alive.

There is an order to activate it. The amazing thing about this short story is that as Jesus walked toward Jairus's daughter, he performed another miracle as he passed by.

The woman in the cloak shows us another kind of faith: she went calmly, communicated silently, and followed through with her actions and beliefs.

Miracles happen in the moment when Jesus thinks, walks, speaks, or moves, at centimeters and over incalculable distances, He is the master of time and space.

Don't limit yourself, go beyond your limits. Jesus accomplished so much in an age so full of hatred and anger because He never remained in the synagogue; many people would have known nothing about Him if He had not gone out and crossed over, He never remained still. The walls of the synagogue couldn't stop Him, couldn't shut Him in; neither trials nor mutterings stopped His purpose.

Let's go beyond our capabilities, we need to look to our soul for incentives that push us to go beyond what our talents or gifts define. Let us be like Him. Never follow me, for He is the only one worthy of imitation.

It's time.

ROAR

ROARRR!!!
R
O
O
A
A
R
R
ROAR

Before we go

Letter to my mother

They say I almost died at birth, but you saved me. Your immense heart knew something was wrong, your spirit heard my cry and your love rescued me. As a fetus, it was already worth the fight because I knew that a queen, a friend and mentor was waiting for me. I couldn't miss my life if you were waiting out there, mom, boss, beautiful, Freckles, old lady, Mrs. Delia, cool. How many nicknames have I given you, my angel? But none of them can ever match what you are worth to me.

To call you mother is an understatement, friend is not enough; to call you beautiful doesn't do you justice, and to call you Delia doesn't fit. To look at you is to see the face of an angel.

I know you will say that this was your "responsibility", that you brought me into the world to love and to care for me, and not for me to "thank" you. But you are wrong: How can I not thank you for carrying me nine months in your womb, enduring such discomfort and pushing my 3.2 kg? Don't go, I haven't finished thanking you yet.

Thank you for reading my favorite story 200 times, for making me more than 6,000 breakfasts, for making my bed every time I woke up next to you, for showing me how to tie my shoes, for wiping my boogers, for turning my legs into pistons. You showed me that hands are meant for embracing, not for punching, that I possess strength and how to use it when necessary.

Your example showed me that life is useless without vision, that love is a pact and a decision. You explained to me that the recipe of life contains courage. You prepared me to forgive the unforgivable, not to exchange peace for money, to turn a house into a home, not to look for excuses, to expand my spirit before my wallet.

Thank you for helping me to accept my mistakes, for not giving up or giving me a break, for giving me the gift of serving, of giving and receiving, and for filling me with the desire to learn. Your lessons made me realize that rebellion requires a purpose and that passion and discipline are worth more than all the other talents put together.

You taught me not to lick my wounds, that I was given this life to give it for others, that dreams are discovered by looking upward. With your words and actions, you gave value to forgiveness, gratitude, honor, faithfulness, meekness, humility, and wisdom.

You blew on the little burns on my skin, nursed my colds, prepared my desserts, defended me in public and lectured me in private; you worked tirelessly to feed me. You made me laugh so much that I got my first wrinkle. When I was afraid, you took me on your lap; you caressed me while I slept. You smiled even when I was sick, you served me the bread from your own mouth, you called me son, and made me a man.

You comforted me when I was broken, you exalted my virtues and polished my character. Today you love me as if I had never been wrong, as when I would turn up the music and afflict your ears with my guitar. You stitched my pants, you urged me to use the subway and to get to where I was going on my own; you stayed awake waiting for me, you grieved my stumbles more than your own, you took me to Disneyland and you hid from me the debt you had taken on for that trip.

You put up with the scoldings of your boss when you left work to take care of me when I was sick, and your kisses would always cure me. If I asked you how you were, you always answered: "I'm fine. God takes care of me." You taught me that you become a millionaire by helping others. I know I could spend days, hours, and even years listing the reasons to thank you.

Thank you, because today I treat my wife like a princess because I was raised by a queen.

Not all superheroes wear capes, mine has wrinkles and moles on her face. Her superpowers include a hug that destroys fear, a kiss that erases sorrow, and a smile that destroys bitterness.

Is it clearer to you now why no name is good enough for you?

Thank you for carrying God's kindness in your fingers.

I love you, Mom.

Letter to an oppressed people

Those of you who have had to leave your homeland, even though every second you miss the smell of your home, the noises of your neighborhood, and the laughter of your grandmother, you should know that you are not alone. You have thousands of human torches that, like watchtowers united from miles around, we send you a sign of hope, because we know that you have gone out to seek reinforcements. You see your homeland bleed and have become numb in the face of human brutality. We are here because the best tool for progress is mutual edification; regardless of nationality or origin, we have all at one time or another felt the need to serve others.

Our land has undergone suffering for a long time. We inhabit a continent that for centuries has received the scourge of generals and warlords, "strong men", who in their weakness have led their nations as if they were their own personal estates. These people have gotten us used to weak institutions and constitutions tailored to their needs, not to ours.

Without having opened a book, they hung their portrait in schools; causing the greatest wounds, they put their name on hospitals. They succeeded each other in bloody revolutions, to which they never sent their own children, and they tore away the freedom granted to us by our forefathers.

A cold wind came up from the south, an icy breath of death and torture; a suffocating mist descended from the Caribbean, a smoke of oppression and misery. Millions left their countries, crossing the Andes or throwing themselves into the sea on fragile rafts, more willing to drown or freeze to death than to tolerate the agony of dying in life.

Once more, there is a surge of fighters moving across the mountains, the isthmus, and the channel, in pursuit of the freedom that was stripped from them. Meanwhile, the new warlords emerge from portraits and turn into photogenic figures, exchanging stern looks for populism and scruffy beards for grandeur. They all use the cheap trick of pitting one against the other. While we hate ourselves, they feed their personal fortunes and keep the poison that has perverted them alive.

They get rich while you suffer, humiliated outside your homeland, and watching it suffer inside. In this world, all it takes is a small spark to overcome the darkness, just ignite your inner self and bring forth the light. Walking in clarity is an act of courage, because transversing obscurity is for people with temperament and character, but above all, with strength and courage.

Fire is created, but only if sparked; its light is the consequence of a reaction that also provides warmth. Today the task is not to illuminate the outside, but the inner world. More than turning on the light, the challenge is to know which light to turn on.

Thank you for resisting the weight of pain, for enduring the indifference, for not giving up and for being hardened in the face of terror. It takes a lot of courage to smile when you are broken inside, and when you have no choice but to leave the place you love or give up your life for its freedom. Thank you for giving us all a deep reason to defend our convictions and value our democracy.

Your job is to make reality a deeper plane, to tell the modern world and warped reality that your dreams are not there to be messed with. Your job is to confront the unhinged irony of pragmatism, and tear down the false image that attempts to export misery everywhere.

Don't stop dreaming: you didn't lose your dreams, they just clouded your vision, but today your vision is back. I am here to tell you that the generation that lost its dreams and struggled in chains will rise up to end slavery. The countries of our earth that suffer oppression will not see their death, but a renaissance. And soon, very soon, you will sleep as God brought you into the world: without fear, without chains, without hunger, and without pain.

Those who had to flee will return to their homes, they will recover their splendor and their light will not be fleeting; from the depths of pain will be born nations that will bring light to the world.

The rulers who today trample on the people with their vulgarities and illusions will know that the most powerful leader is not the one who possesses armies and fortunes, nor the one who enjoys a hundred servants or a thousand women, nor the one who rules over the masses with fear and terror. The most powerful leader in the world is the one who loves others more than himself, the one who conquers without leaving a trail of blood, the one who disarms armies and opens frontiers, the one who traffics in good.

When they meet their downfall due to betrayal from their allies, we will rip off those suits full of medals and reveal the fearful children they always were, who now rely on terror to mask their weakness.

Take a good look at this Mexican whose heart is filled with passion, beating with verses of Rubén Darío and pulsating to the rhythm of Latin music, who tells you that there will always be difficult days, when pain will be paralyzing, but nothing is forever. You could have lost everything these last 10, 20, or 60 years, everything could have been stolen from you, but you still have life to get it all back. Today we will try again, because the time has come to achieve total victory.

The only way to end evil is to be focused on good; there are no boundaries between us. Many will tell you that it's no longer worth fighting for tomorrow, but soon those tears will be rewarded, and those wounds will be transformed into smiles.

It is time to clean up and shake off the dust, to learn that from bad times come good times. You will emerge indestructible, like a diamond.

From now on, you will only talk about victories. And even if life knocks us down, we will stay strong, because nothing and no one can stop a continent that never gives up. Let us kneel down and be driven by it, so that new opportunities may arise and God's blessings may never be held back.

America. Roar, roar. Roar!

This is not a time to be afraid of life, but for life to be afraid of us.

God bless you!

Letter to men

Have you ever imagined what the world would be like without them?

We have different sexes and come in different molds, but one thing is clear to me: we are born male and through males we become men.

Without them our dreams would not exist, without them neither you nor I would know the world around us. Without them we would have grown up malnourished and vapid, without them we would be nothing but smelly cavemen; without them you would not know how to shake hands, and your tears would have no meaning. They demonstrate the perfection of creation, because only in this way could something so akin to love, kindness, mercy, and forgiveness emerge.

We should thank women for bearing us with so much love during childbirth, for being the favorite instrument, for being co-creators of the universal creation, for their recipes and seasonings, for their curves and smiles, for their gray hair and wrinkles. We should thank them for waking us up to go to school, for their cries and moans, for their strength and character, for their dances and touches, for their inventions and complaints. Let us pay tribute to them for their valuable support and for demonstrating wisdom in dealing with people who lack intelligence.

Let us ask for forgiveness in the name of all the men who have hurt, blasphemed, deceived, forgotten, betrayed, used, insulted, beaten... No! Life is not long enough to ask for forgiveness for that. I want a world where each of us walks the earth to honor, love, care for, and bless women.

A great man is not the one who conquers a thousand women in his life, but the one who has only one and conquers her a thousand times, reinventing himself every day, minute by minute, second by second.

A man is not someone who builds a house and abandons it, but someone who builds a house and makes it the home of his family.

Long live women!

Letter to a genius

Your brilliant intellect, your sharp observation, your precise skills, your insatiable thirst for knowledge. You lived between yes and no. I think you are an open valley like the Vinci of Tuscany, heart of the Etruscans. The intricacies of your left-handedness seem to have no limits, you made up for your limited studies with a sharp eye and an inexhaustible imagination. Seeing the birds, you wanted to fly, and you did. You made us fly.

Obsessed with light and optics, symmetry and the height of perfection, uniting art and science. Vegetarian, affable, pleasant, elegant, refined, and sophisticated; you were a nonconformist, a master of the unfinished. Apparently, nothing was alien to you. You were the man who wanted to know everything: to define you as a painter is to diminish you, you are the symbol of universal thought, pure mental alchemy from unity to multiplicity.

You were a brilliant person with both strengths and weaknesses, just like anyone who is ready to pay the price of being framed in the museum of life. Your generosity fed all your friends, rich or poor, between Machiavelli and Botticelli, the Medici and Sforza, the Borgia and your quarrel with Michelangelo.

Thank you for the "Virgin of the Rocks", for the "Portrait of a Musician", for your traces in the "Annunciation", for hiding behind the smile of the "Mona Lisa" and her 77 by 53, there we see you among the "sfumato" that bathes that face of mystery. Thank you for showing us the hardships of "San Jerónimo", the feminine lucidity in the "Lady with an Ermine", for the 24 palms of the Vitruvian Man. I cried when I saw "The Last Supper" in Santa Maria delle Grazie. What a mural in tempera and oil! It feels like you painted it with fury. I can imagine you in Milan looking for a face for Judas, I think you ended up painting the prior instead, in the end they were just as treacherous, weren't they?

Your paintings are not seen, they see us. Not content with such supreme talent, you broke through and excelled in so many different areas: engineer, architect, botanist, musician, poet, anatomist, scientist, sculptor, philosopher, urban planner, paleontologist. To say polymath is an understatement.

You left us giant crossbows, the Tortuga, a horse-head lyre, goggles for diving in the Arno, and even frivolities such as the formula for a blond dye or how to prepare a bath for the Duke's wife. I imagine you walking between Rome, Florence, and Venice, breaking the canons, wearing pink velvet robes, covered in blood, dissecting everything from horses to hair, being the pinnacle of the Renaissance. Your legacy is unquestionable, thousands and thousands of pages crammed with drawings and notes.

Five hundred years after you left us, we are still amazed by your unsolvable enigmas, your dynamo-like questions. Your life and work remain a mystery, we wonder how you could do it all in one life, it makes me want to dive into the Mediterranean with the diving suit you invented.

Your dedication was unwavering and tireless, you never succumbed to idleness and always rejected mediocrity; you abandoned anything that did not contribute to your goal, and you were never swayed by others who tried to convince you to do otherwise. We never admire realists, we never highlight the ordinary. The absurd fail because they are afraid of getting ahead, they do not lose because they always bet on failure; this fear traps them in doubt, which is why they don't dare to give their all.

You never kept your talents to yourself because there is no such thing as small gifts. You showed us that to seek the impossible is to tell reality that we are not to be messed with. You dreamed big and never looked back: you did it no matter what.

We need dreamers like you for this absurd reality. Where are the Leonardos?

Letter to my dad

Today I woke up thinking of you, Dad. I dreamed of you and, for an instant, I thought I could call you, but you are no longer here. Still, I kneel down to talk to you, looking for the answer to that message as a young man that you never answered. I didn't hear your voice, but I heard the voice of my heavenly Father: "Daniel, he is with me and we are both proud of you: You are a good son."

I felt my tears fall and a balm covered my soul. I don't deny that very often I reproached your actions, that I cried and didn't understand your actions. My heart would break just mentioning your name and imagining your face. A few times I could hug you; a few times I could talk to you. You were extremely well balanced, with a temper and firmness such as has rarely been seen. Your character and your strength generated respect: you were solitary, morose, and when you said something, it was tinged with sarcasm.

Your calluses were carved out by the work of those who get their hands dirty and then eat with them. I never saw you wear a suit or tie; instead, you dressed up with two pens and two pencils in your shirt pocket. Engineer and a military man, you were leaving formulas, equations, and poems on napkins and on the back of envelopes. You liked Bob Marley and the first thing you taught me was that the Pythagorean theorem was not created by him. You were an expert in history, you loved birds, they made you believe in God.

You kept your right fist tight because you were determined not to let life bring you down, even with the challenges you faced, including two cancers. Despite this, you continued to work tirelessly, study diligently, and maintain strict discipline, you were a visionary who invented hundreds of products that are still in use all over the world.

Even though you left so recently, your memory is already so precious to me. When the time is right we will have eternity to talk and chat about Sparta and Thermopylae. As I write, my soul drips, leaving puddles between the letters. Forgive me if your little one cries, but if I don't, I'll be flooded inside. I know you won't read these words, but maybe they will be helpful to someone who doesn't have a father in their life.

Alejandro, you are in my blood, in all my veins; your essence lives in me. Your death, rather than leaving me incomplete, ended up making me complete and healing your absence. Today I realize that your remoteness represents a great teaching in my life. In my younger days, I held you responsible for the negative things, but now I credit you with all the positivity in my life that comes from you. No doubt I inherited my courage and resilience from you. I have been educated by your absence. How many absences are there that teach us that love needs to be nurtured, refined, and renewed?

The pain of absence helps us grow, not when we learn to let go of the one who leaves us, but when we let go of the pieces of us that remain attached to them.

I am writing this letter to you in case it reaches the hands of anyone who still feels resentment toward one of their parents, so that they may know that they must forgive once and for all. It may be painful, but it is always better to live in honesty than to pretend out of bitterness. Forgiveness is the key to personal reconciliation, it is the redeeming agent of every wound. The Word commands us to honor our parents in spite of everything—absences, cries, betrayals, failures, and curses—and promises us length of days, wisdom, and glory on this earth.

If this world were a little more forgiving, we would be less attached to it.

I will see you soon. But until that time comes, I will honor your memory by being the best at what I do. Although your eyes will not see these words, I can see them.

I will always love you, Dad.

Your son Daniel

Letter to my wife

My wife, you are my greatest success and greatest blessing. The more truths we speak about God, the more lies they will tell about us; but what does it matter if you, He, and I stand united. Let people keep their wealth, prestige, and acclaim, I see them attain success and renown, whoever they may be, in securing impressive titles, in claiming awards and accolades, whoever they may be, I see their accomplishments in the public sphere, but not in their personal lives.

I have lost some hair, but not the pleasure of hugging you. I have lost business, but not the joy of dedicating myself to you. I have lost pieces of skin, but I still remember the touch of your hands. I have drifted apart from friends, but your memories remain with me. I have missed flights, yet the skies where you carry me still remain. I have lost time, but not the hours in your arms. I have lost a lot, but with you I have gained everything, because I have you, and you love me.

What is life worth if you have no one to lose it for?

You don't need to win, but to lose everything for the other, that's why I insist that the world can have the world, because I prefer you.

Since I cannot love you more, it's like the butterflies that used to flutter in my stomach are now flying in my head. That's why, when they asked me about drugs, I told them about your smile.

You, my wife, my shining star, my ray of sunshine, my friend, my lover, my partner; you are the one I want to be with today, tomorrow, and always. Thinking about infinity excites me. Do you know why? Because it reminds me that we still have so far to go together. I love the springs, the falls, and the nights by your side, the pains are the glory of those of us who understand that we come to this world to love, and you have made me love as God commands me to.

Anyha, I want you to know that it doesn't matter how big or small our home is, or how wide or narrow our room is, as long as we can look into each other's eyes, and know that infinity lies within our gazes.

See how the sun lingers, refusing to set, so that I can continue to take in your beauty.

Danny

Letter to hypocrites

Stop asking what my religion is. You will not be able to discourage me by saying that our beliefs are different; the more you try to harm those who do not share your beliefs, the more I will strive to alleviate their suffering; the more you divide people based on their thoughts, the more I aim to connect science with spirituality, reason with compassion; the more you exploit the less fortunate, the more I will support those with a prosperous mindset rather than those with a desperate mind; the more you censure those who do not worship God the way you do, the more I will praise the marginalized and those who have failed in spirituality.

You demand that I show my fruits, meanwhile you rot without ripening. I work hard to imitate Christ, not those who call themselves Christians. He said that His followers would be known for their love and mercy, not for their protest banners, snap judgments, and harmful confrontation to the culture that makes them uncomfortable.

You preach eternity, but you live as if you never want to reach it. While you want people to call you "religious", I expect nothing more than to embrace Christ, to represent Him to the fullest and to live in Him intensely. I want to be a light in the world, not the star of a church; I want people to follow their dreams, not mine. I am one of those who do not qualify to follow Jesus, but yet I still do. I will return your contradictions with kisses.

You shield yourself in the Bible without taking refuge in it. You see it as a wall that excludes, and not as the immense hall that welcomes those who need its protection. Quoting verses and shouting "the Bible says" will get you nowhere if you don't apply it to yourself first. It will not be enough to tell the world that according to Matthew this, or according to Luke that; instead of condemning those who do not know it, be the living Bible for those who do not read it.

God is greater than a simple concept, than a label; God is much more than a tradition preserved in a metal building. God is God for everyone and not just for those who think like you. Stop separating the world between religious and secular, stop isolating yourself in a bubble so as not to be infected. It's very easy to think you are enlightened when in reality you are walking in the light of others.

Modern prejudices, post-Enlightenment, and the gross ignorance with which you regard the Scriptures have led you to trivialize the Word and to turn it into magic cartoons, far from the majesty of its wisdom, which must be studied, but, first of all, must be lived.

Stop editing my language. I don't masquerade as perfect. I am not one of those who speak in fancy languages without mastering their own. I know that at times my words can be grandiose, but I prefer them to your preaching of hatred. I think there is no summit that cannot be reached on your knees.

Every day I face my ego and fight to dominate it, although sometimes I lose the battle. I join the incongruous, those who still have a thousand wounds to heal. I too have been a stumbling block in someone else's path. This work that you see is not yet finished, it is still being perfected, because I am not the potter who sculpts it, but the clay that is molded by the Artisan of the cosmos.

I believe in unconditional love, in loving our enemies; I believe in a love that does not include a list of tests to be fulfilled. I don't stop to see if someone deserves my hug or not. Only afterwards will I know if I did the right thing or not.

I give my imperious voice to those who fear to shout their own. I don't intend to form an army of sheep, there are already many sheep that bleat: help me, take care of me, pray for me. I see that there are too many who fleece their flock instead of shearing it. This world does not need more sheep, it needs leaders willing to live at the forefront on all flanks, the call is to be bold, not passive.

Meanwhile, you refuse to take on that battle, you justify yourself by saying that from your trench you do what you can. The bull always looks tame from the sidelines. Anyone can shout "Olé!" from the comfort of the stands.

You rebuke my use of language, but you change the words "love" and "mercy" to "apostate" and "false prophet". Victory lies between what you think and what you feel, the struggle between what you want and what you do, the glory between why and what for. No one is going to lock up those responsible for your insecurities.

There is no sadder story than the one of the person whose life was a blank page, but whose cowardice allowed others to fill the page for them.

Stop blaming me for what I am. I warn you that false people will be crushed by truth. Shut up if you're going to judge, shut up if you're going to criticize.

The evil man blames God.

The religious man blames the devil.

The Pharisee blames money.

The legalist blames the libertarian.

The fool does not know who to blame.

The proud blames others, and in the grave of the proud is buried the fool.

Look at the good, look for the good, don't stop improving and growing. Give me your hand and let us not stop doing good, let us not use our life for thinking and wishing evil, let us follow with wisdom those paths that rob us of peace; let us take the best of people and of those around us, let us fill ourselves with joy, let us be a little "less bad" and a little "more good"; and if you don't know how to be good, don't worry, for there is also a place for you at the heavenly table.

Let us seek prosperity from the inside out, but above all let us seek the best for others and share our bread with all those who need some. Be wise in your mistakes and humble in your successes, love yourself in the dark and don't be dazzled by the light.

I don't know what your life purpose is, but if you still don't know what it is, go and serve others. I assure you that there you will find an inexhaustible mine of peace, joy, and happiness.

The next time you see someone empty, fill them with love, not judgment.